T0360686

Managing Organizational Complexities with Digital Enablement in China

A Casebook

Series on Innovation and Knowledge Management

Series Editor: Suliman Hawamdeh   ISSN: 1793-1533
           (University of North Texas)

Published*

*The complete list of the published volumes in the series can be found at
http://www.worldscientific.com/series/sikm

Series on Innovation and Knowledge Management – Vol. 13

Managing Organizational Complexities with Digital Enablement in China

A Casebook

Edited by

PAN Shan-Ling

University of New South Wales, Australia

World Scientific

NEW JERSEY · LONDON · SINGAPORE · BEIJING · SHANGHAI · HONG KONG · TAIPEI · CHENNAI

Published by

World Scientific Publishing Co. Pte. Ltd.

5 Toh Tuck Link, Singapore 596224

USA office: 27 Warren Street, Suite 401-402, Hackensack, NJ 07601

UK office: 57 Shelton Street, Covent Garden, London WC2H 9HE

Library of Congress Cataloging-in-Publication Data
Managing organizational complexities with digital enablement in China : a casebook / [edited] by Shan-Ling Pan.
    pages cm. -- (Series on innovation and knowledge management, ISSN 1793-1533 ; vol. 13)
    Includes index.
    ISBN 978-9814623148
    1. Information technology--China--Management--Case studies. 2. Management--China--Case studies. I. Pan, Shan-Ling.
    HC430.I55M36 2015
    658'.050951--dc23
                                              2014040555

British Library Cataloguing-in-Publication Data
A catalogue record for this book is available from the British Library.

In-house Editors: Dipasri Sardar/Rajni Gamage

Typeset by Stallion Press
Email: enquiries@stallionpress.com

Printed in Singapore

Contents

About the Editor

Dr. Shan L. Pan is Professor of Information Systems, Technology and Management, UNSW Australia Business School.

Dr. Pan's research work has been published in Information Systems Research, *Journal of AIS; Management Information Systems Quarterly Executive; Journal of the Academy of Marketing Studies; IEEE Transaction on Engineering Management; Journal of the American Society for Information Science and Technology; IEEE Transactions on Systems, Man, and Cybernetics; IEEE Transactions on Information Technology in Biomedicine; European Journal of Operational Research; OMEGA: International Journal of Management Science; Communications of ACM; Information and Organization; Journal of Strategic Information Systems; Journal of Organizational Computing and Electronic Commerce; European Journal of Information Systems; Decision Support Systems; Journal of the Operational Research Society; DATA BASE for Advances in Information Systems*; and among others.

Dr. Shan L. Pan's research interests include the strategic use and impacts of Information Communication and Technology (ICT) on business and social innovation. He has conducted more than 50 in-depth studies on state-owned enterprises, commercial organizations, villages and non-profit organizations in China, India, Malaysia, Singapore, Taiwan and Thailand.

Professor Pan has research interests in the socio-organizational processes that underlie the interaction between information technology and their human and organizational contexts. His primary research focuses on the recursive interaction of organizations and ICT, with particular emphasis on organizational issues such as work practices, cultures, structures, decision-making, change, strategy implementation that often require qualitative research methods.

About the Contributors

Barney Tan
Business Information Systems
The University of Sydney Business School
Email: barney.tan@sydney.edu.au

Barney Tan is a Senior Lecturer in Business Information Systems at the University of Sydney Business School. His research interests include strategic IT management, qualitative research methods, enterprise systems and e-commerce. His work has been published in well-regarded academic journals and conferences including the *IEEE Transactions on Engineering Management*, the *European Management Journal*, the *International Conference on Information Systems*, and the *Academy of Management Meeting*.

Miao Cui
Department of Technological Economics and Management
Faculty of Management and Economics, Dalian University of Technology
Li Gong Road No. 2, Gaoxin District
Dalian, China 116024
Email: cuimiao@dlut.edu.cn

Miao Cui is currently Associate Professor in the Department of Technological Economics and Management, Faculty of Management and Economics, Dalian University of Technology. Her research interests include innovation management and IT-enabled innovation.

Zheng Wang

Case Writer
Centre for Management Practice
Singapore Management University
Email: zackwang@smu.edu.sg

Dr. Zheng Wang (Zack) is a Case Writer (senior manager) for the Centre for Management Practice at Singapore Management University. He received a Ph.D. in Information Systems from the National University of Singapore. Prior to this, he earned a Masters degree in Analysis, Design and Management of Information Systems from London School of Economics and Political Science and a BSc in Computer Science from University of Warwick, UK. Zack has five years' experience in qualitative research and conducted more than 12 case studies relating to IT strategy and outsourcing topics in multiple countries such as Singapore and China. His work has been published in leading journals such as IEEE transactions on engineering management and information & management.

Taohua Ouyang

Department of Business Administration
School of Economics and Management
Bei Hang University
China
Email: taohuaouyang@hotmail.com

Taohua Ouyang is currently Professor in the Department of Business Administration, School of Economics and Management, Bei Hang University. She has been tracing for research on a number of Chinese enterprises for many years such as the Haier Group. Her research interests include strategic management, international and diversified management, and human resource management. Dr. Ouyang has conducted and published more than 20 academic papers and 4 management books on Chinese and Japanese organizations.

Carmen Mei Ling Leong

Department of Information Systems
School of Computing, National University of Singapore
15 Computing Drive
Singapore 117418
Email: leongml@nus.edu.sg

Carmen Mei Ling Leong is a Ph.D. candidate of Information Systems at the School of Computing at the National University of Singapore. She obtained her M.Sc. in Information Systems from NUS in 2007. Her research interest is in the area of strategic IT issues, IT-enabled social innovation, and IT-enabled embeddedness.

Jenson Goh

Department of Information Systems
School of Computing, National University of Singapore
15 Computing Drive
Singapore 117418
Email: jensongoh@nus.edu.sg

Jenson Goh is a part-time doctoral candidate in the Department of Information Systems, School of Computing at the National University of Singapore since 2007. He obtained his Bachelor of Science degree in Computer Science and Master of Science degree in Computer Science from NUS in 1997 and 2000 respectively. He started his Ph.D. hugely due to his hunger for knowledge in the area of strategic management. While he does have many opportunities to pursue this interest in strategic management on the job, he is not satisfied with it and wants to learn more about this knowledge in a rigorous research environment. His research interests include (but are not limited to) Strategic Management, Business-IT alignment, and Enterprise Agility. Jenson's full-time job is a Senior IT

Manager in Computer Centre, National University of Singapore. He heads the Enterprise Architecture Team and the Strategic UTown Admission System Team. Jenson is also a Resident Fellow in King Edward VII Hall of Residence, National University of Singapore where he is part of the Hall Senior Management.

Mei-Yun Zuo
Department of Economic Information Management
School of Information, Renmin University of China
No. 59, Zhongguancun Road, Haidian District, Beijing
China 100872
Email: zuomy@ruc.edu.cn

Mei-Yun Zuo is Professor and Associate Dean, School of Information, Renmin University, China. He also is an associate chair of Chinese Information Economics Society. He received his Ph.D. degree from School of Management, Harbin Institute of Technology, Harbin, China. His academic interests include information system adoption, knowledge management, the impact of IT on the elderly, etc. Dr. Zuo was a winner of Ten Outstanding Teachers' Reward from Renmin University of China (2006). His teaching interests include IT Project Management, Knowledge Management, and Enterprise Information Management.

Derek Wenyu Du
Department of Management Science and Engineering
Renmin University, China
Email: duwenyu@rbs.org.cn

Derek Wenyu Du's research interests include IT outsourcing, Organizational Ambidexterity, and Boundary Spanning. He has published several papers at International Conferences on Information Systems (ICIS). His recent paper "Boundary Spanning by Design: Insights from a Vendor Perspective" has won the runner-up best paper award at ICIS 2010.

Adela Chen

Assistant Professor
Department of Computer Information Systems
Colorado State University
Rockwell Hall, 32 United States
Colorado State University
Email: adelachen@business.colostate.edu

Dr. Adela Chen is an Assistant Professor of Information Systems at Colorado State University. She received her PhD in Management Information Systems from Terry College of Business, University of Georgia. Dr. Chen's research interests are in technology-mediated interruptions and multitasking in human computer interaction, understanding the impact of information technology on users' work and personal life, and understanding the role of information systems in environmental sustainability. Dr. Chen's research has appeared in MIS Quarterly, Information and Management, Journal of Strategic Information Systems, and the IEEE Transactions on Engineering Management.

Wayne Huang

Management Information Systems College of Business
Ohio University
United States
Email: huangw@ohio.edu

Wayne Huang is a Professor of MIS at the College of Business, Ohio University. He received his Ph.D. degree from the National University of Singapore. He has published more than 100 academic papers.

Tzu-Chuan Chou

National Taiwan University of Science and Technology
43, Sec. 4, Keelung Road, Taipei 106, Taiwan
Email: tcchou@mail.ntust.edu.tw

Tzu-Chuan Chou is Professor in the Department of Information Management at National Taiwan University of Science and Technology. Dr. Chou received his Ph.D. in Information management from Warwick Business School, the University of Warwick, UK, in 1999. Dr. Chou joined the School of Management, NTUST in 2005 and teaches several managerial courses. Dr. Chou's current research focuses on the IT/IS outsourcing, IT management, knowledge management, and E-government.

Peiying Huang

Management Consultant
Sequoia Group Pte. Ltd. (Singapore)
winston.huang@sequoia.com.sg

Dr. Peiying Huang (Winston) is a management consultant at Sequoia Group Pte. Ltd. He received a Ph.D. in Information Systems from the National University of Singapore. Prior to this, he earned his Bachelor of Science in Software Engineering from the South China University of Technology in 2009. Winston has studied four famous Chinese organizations (i.e. Haier, JD.com, Tecent, and Jeanswest) in the past four years. His research interests include IT entrepreneurship, IT innovation and IT-enabled agility. Winston has published his work in leading journals such as European Journal of Information Systems and International Journal of Information Management.

Mao Mao

Department of Information Systems
School of Computing, National University of Singapore
15 Computing Drive
Singapore 117418
Email: maomao@comp.nus.edu.sg

Mao Mao is currently an M.Sc. candidate of Information Systems at the School of Computing at the National University of Singapore. She obtained her B.B.A in the School of Business, Nanjing University in 2011. Her study includes IT strategy and organizational culture issues, and IT-enabled social innovation.

Elaine Jing Chen
Department of Information Systems
School of Computing, National University of Singapore
15 Computing Drive
Singapore 117418
Email: elaine.chen.jing@gmail.com

Elaine Jing Chen is a Ph.D. candidate of the Department of Information Systems in the School of Computing at National University of Singapore (NUS). Her research interests include IT-enabled organizational routine, and other IT-related managerial issues. She has published her work in journals such as Information and Management, and International Journal of Information Management, as well as conferences such as International Conference on Information Systems (ICIS) 2010 and Hawaii International Conference on Systems Science (HICSS-44).

Hui Wang
BeiHang University
XueYuan Road
No.37, HaiDian District
Beijing, China
Email: 15811385621@139.com

Hui Wang is currently a MBA student at Beihang University. Her research interest is strategic management.

Say Yen Teoh
School of Business IT and Logistics
RMIT University
445 Swanston Street
SAB Building 80, Level 8
Melbourne VIC 3000
Australia
Email: sayyen.teoh@rmit.edu.au

Say Yen Teoh received the Ph.D. degree in information systems from the National University of Singapore (NUS). She is currently a senior lecturer at the School of Business IT and Logistics and a member of the Health Innovation Research Institute (HIRI) at RMIT University, Australia. Her professional interest is to explore the design, implementation, and evaluation of the Enterprise Systems, Health Informatics, E-Health and Enterprise Systems. Her research has been published in various journals such as *Journal of Global Information Management; Information Systems Frontiers; Database for Advances in Information Systems; Journal of Information Technology Management; Journal of Systems and Information Technology; International Journal on E-Health and Medical Communications; International Journal of Actor-Network Theory and Technological Innovation; Journal of Enterprise Information Management.*

Xi Chen

Department of Management Science and Engineering
School of Management
Zhejiang University
China
Email: chen_xi@zju.edu.cn

Xi Chen is an Associate Professor of department of management science and engineering. He has been awarded titles as Qiu Shi Young Scholar (from ZJU), Qian Jiang Talent (from Zhejiang Province), and Zhi Jiang Young Social Science Scholar (from Zhejiang Province). He obtained his Ph.D. from the University of Hong Kong, MS from National University of Singapore, and his BS from Fudan University. His research interests include health care information systems, mobile commerce, business intelligence and data mining. He has published paper in international journals such as *Decision Support Systems, European Journal of Operational Research, Journal of the American Society for Information Science and Technology, Journal of Global Information Management, and Electronic Commerce Research and Applications.* He is an Associate Editor of Information & Management and a member of editorial advisory board of Internet Research.

Preface

Since the introduction of computers into commercial use in the 1950s, information technology (IT) has presented many opportunities for organizations to enhance or transform their products, services, markets, work processes, and business relationships. The potential of IT to transform private and public organizations has thus been a persistent theme in both management and information systems literature and managerial practices. This book provides organizational and managerial views on adopting emerging technologies for organizational transformation. 17 in-depth case studies documenting experiences and lessons learned in organizations from China were presented in this teaching casebook.

With a regional focus, this book provides the much-needed insights into the adoption and implementation of emerging technologies in China. These case materials can provide useful practical lessons for practitioners when planning and implementing similar business systems. The cases can also act as constructive road maps for classroom teaching and discussions. Each case is set up independently, so that the cases may be studied and discussed in any sequence.

It is hoped that this casebook will bridge the gap in Information Systems literature — lacking the empirical case materials from China — and be the catalyst to elicit more research and teaching materials contextualized in the China context.

1

Alibaba.com

Barney Tan

Organizational Background

According to the latest statistics from the web traffic tracking agency Compete, Alibaba is one of the world's largest B2B e-commerce portals with over 2.6 million unique visitors per month. Alibaba's business centers on providing a trading platform that connects international buyers to millions of small and medium-sized enterprises (SMEs) in China that supply a kaleidoscopic array of products, ranging from agricultural products to aircraft parts. But since its inception, Alibaba has diversified into a wide range of businesses ranging from a consumer-to-consumer (C2C) online auction website (Taobao), an Internet portal (Yahoo China), an online review website for lifestyle products and services (Koubei), and an online advertising trading platform (Alimama). Incidentally, according to the web traffic tracking agency Alexa, these spin-offs, together with Alibaba, are all among the top 100 most popular websites in China, a considerable achievement that belies Alibaba's humble origins.

The initial manifestation of Alibaba was ChinaPages.com. Launched in April 1995, ChinaPages was a small e-business that provided website development and indexing services to local enterprises. At the time, there were no commercial Internet service providers in China and the general population was unaware of the existence of the Internet. Yet, led by Jack Ma, the iconic founder of ChinaPages and later Alibaba, ChinaPages was able to convince many Chinese firms of the business potential of the Internet and subsequently, to engage its services. For approximately US$3,000, ChinaPages would translate the corporate and product information of their clients into English and send the translation to collaborators in the US who would develop and launch websites based on the information. And as commercial internet access became available over time, ChinaPages developed the technical capabilities required for website development and eventually, took over the role from their US collaborators as well.

In 1997, ChinaPages was merged with a local competitor but due to differences in strategic vision, Jack Ma and eight members of the core development team left the organization. Because of their experience in e-commerce, they were eventually roped in by the Chinese government to develop ChinaMarket, an e-government portal for global firms to locate products, services, and business opportunities in China. It was the experience of managing both ChinaPages and ChinaMarket, which led to the realization that China's enormous SME market would benefit immensely from the global exposure afforded by the Internet, and back then, there were no B2B platforms that catered exclusively to Chinese SMEs as the costs of joining a B2B platform were prohibitive. With this critical insight, Jack Ma and his core team left ChinaMarket and returned to Hangzhou with the dream of establishing a B2B e-commerce portal that connected the hundreds of thousands of Chinese SMEs to the world. This led to the founding of Alibaba in March 1999 and at the time, Alibaba was operating out of Jack Ma's apartment and the entire development team drew a salary of only US$73 a month. Yet, within a short span of 9 years, Alibaba has become a publicly listed multinational corporation with over 10,000 employees worldwide and an annual revenue of US$207 million. Alibaba's vibrant and populous DBE was cited by numerous informants as the primary driver of enterprise agility, which, in turn, was crucial to its phenomenal success.

To illustrate, a senior executive at Alibaba attested to the integral role of its DBE:

"Our ecosystem is the key to our success... We have a close relationship with our (ecosystem) members... we know their needs and we are able to meet their needs quickly and effectively... this strengthens our members and enables them to contribute to the collective good... It is a virtuous cycle. When the ecosystem prospers, everyone (within the ecosystem) prospers..."

The case of Alibaba reveals three pertinent themes: (1) the antecedents of ecosystem development manifested in the strategies and ecosystem role of Alibaba, (2) the nature of ecosystem development, and (3) the consequences of ecosystem development centered on the facilitation of enterprise agility. From the emergent data, it became readily apparent that Alibaba underwent three distinct phases, adopting different strategies and ecosystem roles in each phase, which resulted in different forms of ecosystem development, with correspondingly distinct implications for enterprise agility.

Leveraging Firm-Specific Resources and Capabilities (1999–2004)

In the first phase from 1999 to 2004, Alibaba's business objectives were centered on establishing itself as the *de facto* platform for B2B e-commerce in China. Competitive imitation was rampant in the rapidly developing Chinese e-commerce industry then, and Alibaba had to act quickly to preempt potential competitors from imitating its business model. Accordingly, Alibaba enacted a number of strategies that were broadly aligned with three strategic thrusts. First, Alibaba took advantage of its unique insight of the unmet needs of Chinese SMEs and structured value creation towards meeting those needs. Second, Alibaba exploited its superior technical capabilities, developed from its experience in operating ChinaPages and ChinaMarket, to differentiate itself from the existing B2B portals in China (e.g., HC360, EasyTrade). Third, Alibaba leveraged its intimate knowledge of local SMEs and incorporated the nuances of Chinese business practices into its transactional processes to differentiate itself from the global B2B portals (e.g., allactiontrade, eceurope, MFGTrade). The collective consequence of these strategic thrusts is a unique value proposition targeted at fulfilling the needs of the immense SME market, which served to attract many Chinese SMEs to join Alibaba's business ecosystem.

In addition, as many of the SMEs lacked the technical capabilities to go online, Alibaba took on the role of a service provider within the ecosystem, helping to collate, organize, publish and promote the corporate and product information of its members on their website. This enabled the SMEs to participate meaningfully in the ecosystem and consequently, benefit from the ubiquitous exposure afforded by the Internet. By providing a unique value proposition and lowering the barriers of participation, Alibaba was able to attract a myriad of SMEs to attain self-sustaining critical mass, and entrench itself at the center of value creation within the DBE. Its centrality in the network, in turn, enhanced Alibaba's ability to sense its customers' needs as Alibaba was able to collect feedback directly from the other entities within the ecosystem. Moreover, as Alibaba's organizational actions were enacted at the center of the network, its actions impacted the entire business ecosystem concurrently, which enabled a quicker response to its customers' needs. The key organizational strategies and ecosystem role adopted by Alibaba, the nature of ecosystem development, and the underlying mechanism through which ecosystem development translates to enterprise agility in Phase 1 are summarized in Table 1.

Acquiring New Organizational Capabilities (2005–2006)

Having established a firm dominance over the Chinese B2B e-commerce market, Alibaba began to realize that the biggest threat to its business came not from the existing B2B e-commerce portals, but rather from massive Internet portals such as Baidu and Google. This is because global firms looking for products, services, and business opportunities from Chinese partners and vice versa, can potentially find them by searching on these Internet portals, disintermediating Alibaba

Table 1. How Alibaba's Ecosystem was Developed and Leveraged in Phase 1 (1999–2004)

Key Organizational Strategies

Leverage unique insight of unmet needs in Chinese SME Market	"We were the first to cater exclusively to the needs of SMEs. As a result, our networking platform, the trust supporting mechanisms we used, and our payment systems were all geared towards meeting the needs of this particular segment. This was what differentiated us from the other B2B platforms in the beginning." — Vice-President (VP) of Customer Relations
Exploit superior technical capabilities developed from prior experience	"The experience from managing ChinaPages (and later ChinaMarket) was instrumental to Alibaba's (initial) success. It was here that they picked up the technical skills of website development and learnt what it took to run a B2B e-commerce portal... In terms of technical capabilities, Alibaba's platform was clearly superior to its competitors." — Industry Insider
Took advantage of its intimate knowledge of Chinese business practices	"There were three factors that differentiated us from our foreign competitors. First, we provided tools like 'Wangwang' (an instant messenger system that allowed transacting parties to haggle over prices) and 'Alipay' (an escrow service that helped mitigate the greater mistrust of online transactions among Chinese firms). Second, we provided our services free of charge. Third, our websites were designed to suit to our Chinese culture." — Senior Manager for Strategic Planning

Ecosystem Role

Service provider	"Many of our members did not know much about e-commerce. But they had posted their corporate and product information on trade-oriented electronic Bulletin Board Systems (BBS)... We helped to collate, organize and publish the relevant information on our website... we organized the information by product category and provided search functionality to lower the cost of finding the information. Lastly, we helped to create awareness for our members... we went to different websites to promote Alibaba, telling people that business opportunities and all kinds of products from all over the globe can be found on our website..." — General Manager (GM) of Alibaba B2B

(Continued)

Table 1. (*Continued*)

Nature of Ecosystem Development	
Development of a self-sustaining DBE with Alibaba at the core	"We attracted many SMEs as well as individual users. As the number of our ecosystem members increased, so did the variety of products on our website... We were positioned at the center of the ecosystem... the ecosystem was dependent on us for survival for we were the infrastructure providers, and the possibility of sustaining our growth was very good."
	— Senior Scientist

Consequences of Ecosystem Development	
Enhanced sense-and-response capabilities	"Our position (at the center of the ecosystem) helps us to effectively sense and respond to the needs of our customers. We can obtain feedback directly from our customers, and this gives us a good feel of what is happening on the ground... By responding to the feedback and acting at our end, the rest of the ecosystem benefits from our actions as well..."
	— GM of Alibaba

from the process of transaction. Consequently, Alibaba began to move in a new strategic direction in 2005. The new strategic direction was characterized by the aggressive acquisition of new organizational capabilities in preparation for the inevitable conflict with the Internet portals in the near future.

First, Alibaba acquired search engine capabilities with the acquisition of Yahoo China in October 2005. The strategic intent behind the acquisition is to create a business-oriented search engine and isolate the members of its DBE from Internet portals such as Google or Baidu. To date, most of the information published on the Alibaba network can no longer be accessed by third-party search engines. Second, in October 2006, Alibaba acquired Koubei.com, one of the most popular online portals for the review of lifestyle products and services, such as restaurants, hair salons, and hotels. Alibaba's management felt that the acquisition of Koubei would strengthen the sense of community within the ecosystem by enabling its members to "work, spend, and play" on Alibaba, and facilitate greater interaction between ecosystem members by encouraging them to spend more time on the Alibaba network.

In addition, with exponential increases in the size of the ecosystem each year, Alibaba had over 10 million registered members by 2005, and as ecosystem members became more experienced and savvy in the use of Internet technologies, it became neither feasible nor necessary for Alibaba to continue providing "hands-on" services for its ecosystem members. Relinquishing its "hands-on" approach was potentially problematic as Alibaba could run the risk of disintermediation. But eventually, Alibaba's role in the ecosystem evolved into that of a platform provider, creating value by supplying the mechanisms for ecosystem members to exchange information, to interact, and to transact with each other, instead of involving itself directly in these activities.

By acquiring Yahoo China, Alibaba was able to demarcate the boundaries of the DBE and consolidate its position at the center of the ecosystem. In addition, by acquiring Koubei and taking on the backend role of a platform provider, thereby relinquishing direct control over its ecosystem members, Alibaba enabled richer and more frequent interactions between members, which facilitated the formation of informal, autonomous networks within the ecosystem. This in turn, enhanced enterprise agility as Alibaba was able to move beyond simply sensing and responding to expressed customer needs, to monitoring and analyzing the interactions between its members to anticipate and predict future and unexpressed needs. The key strategies and ecosystem role of Alibaba, the nature of ecosystem development, and the underlying mechanism through which ecosystem development translates to enterprise agility in Phase 2 are summarized in Table 2.

Developing Ecosystem Capabilities (2007–Present)

The capability acquisition/development strategies of Alibaba led to performance gains that outstripped all initial expectations. Between 2005 and 2006, Alibaba registered an 88.1% increase in revenue, an astounding 212% increase in net profits, and an 80.1% growth in terms of the number of registered members. The phenomenal success of the strategies of this phase made Alibaba's management more keenly aware

Table 2. How Alibaba's Ecosystem was Developed and Leveraged in Phase 2 (2005–2006)

Key Organizational Strategies	
Acquisition of search engine capabilities (Yahoo China)	"With our acquisition of Yahoo China, we are priming ourselves for the inevitable conflict with search engines like Baidu… By integrating e-commerce (Alibaba) with the Internet portal (Yahoo China), search engine capabilities with synchronous communications (Wangwang Instant Messenger), we can increase the stickiness, breadth and depth of our business… Currently, most of the information published on our network have been sealed off from (third party search engines like) Baidu." — Communications Manager of Yahoo Koubei
Acquisition of community-building capabilities (Koubei)	"Koubei represents the initiative to integrate lifestyle services with e-commerce … and represents a step towards the development of search and community-building tools. Our investment in Koubei strings together all our disparate businesses, allowing our ecosystem members to work, spend and play on the Alibaba network." — Communications Manager of Yahoo Koubei

Ecosystem Role	
Platform provider	"Alibaba became a platform provider; providing mechanisms for its members to interact and transact, and no longer had to be directly involved in the transactions. Alibaba served as an platform for exchanging information, communications and interaction, as well as transaction. With Yahoo and Koubei, Alibaba was also the platform for members to search for and review one another." — VP of Research and Training

Nature of Ecosystem Development	
Formation of networks within the ecosystem as a result of enhanced interaction between ecosystem members	"By integrating the largest and most vibrant lifestyle portal in China (Koubei) with the advanced Internet capabilities, large user base and global search capabilities of Yahoo (China), we are able to advance in terms of volume, convenience, trustworthiness and stickiness. In addition, both Yahoo (China) and Koubei encourage interactions and the formation of bonds between our members, helping the SMEs and individual users on our network to live, grow, develop and create leading-edge networks (between themselves)." — Communications Manager of Yahoo Koubei

(Continued)

Table 2. (*Continued*)

Consequences of Ecosystem Development	
Ability to predict and anticipate customer needs	"The development of Alibaba (acquisition of Yahoo China and Koubei) emerged spontaneously and was not the result of systematic planning... By allowing our members to interact with one another and form their own networks, we can collect data on their interactions and transactions, analyze the data to detect patterns or opportunities, and share our results with the entire organization." — VP of Research and Training

of the advantages of an organic, self-organizing ecosystem. Soon after, an ecosystem-oriented mentality took hold within the collective organizational consciousness and provided the foundation for a new strategic direction that began in 2007.

The new strategic direction is manifested in the enactment of two key organizational strategies. First, at the start of 2007, Alibaba launched Aliloan, an initiative in partnership with the Industrial and Commercial Bank of China and the China Construction Bank to help SMEs with limited assets or credit history secure financing for business expansion based on their transaction histories and credibility ratings at Alibaba. Second, in November 2007, Alibaba launched Alimama, a trading platform for online advertising space to enhance the ecosystem capability for online marketing and generating online advertising revenue. The overarching objective of these strategies is to foster a healthy DBE by enhancing the organizational capabilities of the other entities in its ecosystem. In doing so, ecosystem members are able to contribute more to networked value creation, which enhances the overall competitiveness of the ecosystem and benefits Alibaba in the long run.

Moreover, driven by the new ecosystem-oriented mentality, Alibaba's role within the ecosystem evolved into that of a utility-computing service provider (see Carr 2008; Ross and Westerman 2004) with the launch of Alisoft in January 2007. Alisoft is an online software portal based on a Software as a Service (SaaS) model. The purpose of Alisoft is to develop and provide its ecosystem members with a comprehensive suite of low-cost, user-friendly web-based enterprise applications (EA) to meet their business IT needs. With its new strategies and ecosystem role, Alibaba was able to foster symbiotic relationships between entities including itself, within the ecosystem, and channel the resources and actions of individual entities towards the shared objectives of the ecosystem. In this spirit of symbiotism, ecosystem members were engaged in the co-production of innovations, which gives rise to an advanced form of enterprise agility as the innovations are developed and tailor-made for the customers of Alibaba by the customers themselves. The key organizational strategies and ecosystem role adopted by Alibaba, the nature of ecosystem development, and the underlying mechanism through which ecosystem development translates to enterprise agilityin Phase 3 are summarized in Table 3.

Table 3. How Alibaba's Ecosystem was Developed and Leveraged in Phase 3 (2007–Present)

Key Organizational Strategies

Enhance ecosystem business expansion capabilities (Aliloan)	"Alibaba has kept a comprehensive record of all our members' transactions for many years. We can use this to track how the money is used before, during, and after the loan to minimize the costs of filtering the credit-worthy enterprises for the banks... Aliloan is especially important in helping SMEs grow their business as it is difficult for them to obtain loans through conventional channels, and they cannot provide mortgages or guarantees."
	— Alibaba Senior Executive
Enhance ecosystem capability for online marketing and generating online advertising revenue (Alimama)	"After opening a web store, many of Alibaba's members, especially the larger establishments and the 'power sellers' on Taobao have two needs: To promote their store, which implies the need to buy advertisement space, and to sell advertisement space. (They will ask) 'Can I convert my web traffic into revenue?' Our existing services didn't cater to their needs...' This led to the launch of Alimama (an online advertising trading platform)... Alimama is different from Google's or Baidu's advertising programs. It is based on a whole new model."
	— Alimama Senior Manager

(Continued)

Table 3. (*Continued*)

Ecosystem Role	
Utility computing service provider	"Alibaba provides everything an e-merchant needs to run a business. We provide the platform... (as well as) applications and online tools (on Alisoft), allowing them to start their business easily with minimal capital investment. It's like in a village... we have dug the well for everyone... Our business users can use our various platforms to gain access to the SaaS services they need, and they are charged according to usage...We hope to provide for all their needs, such that all anyone needs is a computer to become an e-merchant." — Alisoft Senior Manager
Nature of Ecosystem Development	
Formation of symbiotic relationships between ecosystem members	"By providing services and opportunities to the 'bit players' in our ecosystem, they attract more 'bit players' into the ecosystem... With a very large volume of these small players working synergistically for the collective good of the ecosystem, Alibaba's profitability increases, and we have more resources to invest in enhancing our service platforms... This virtuous cycle results in a healthy ecosystem that is beneficial for all ecosystem members." — VP of Operations
Consequences of Ecosystem Development	
Co-production of innovations	"Many third-party applications developers joined our ecosystem to develop software for Alisoft... Some of our B2B and C2C members used the open-source platform to develop their own applications. These applications include VOIP applications, video conferencing software, wireless telephony applications, website management systems, electronic ID services, and many others... The applications are all available on Alisoft. Alisoft is like a software supermarket, and our users can pick and choose the applications they need." — Alibaba Senior Executive

References

Carr, N. *The Big Switch: Rewiring the World from Edison to Google*. W.W. Norton, New York, NY, 2008.

Ross, J.W. and Westerman, G. "Preparing for utility computing: The role of IT architecture and relationship management," *IBM Systems Journal* (43:1) 2004, pp. 5–19.

Discussion Questions

1. In the initial phase, what are the specific strategic resources and capabilities that the focal company, i.e., Alibaba, should hold in order to establish centrality and attain critical mass? Also, what role did Alibaba play in this phrase? What enterprise agility was achieved by Alibaba in this phase?

2. In the second phase, Alibaba was centered on the acquisition/development of search engine (i.e., Yahoo China) and community building (i.e., Koubei) capabilities. What is the purpose of these actions? What is the difference between the ecosystem role played by Alibaba in Phase one and that played in phase two? What factors do you think push this role change?

3. What strategy did Alibaba adopt in the third phase? What is the purpose for applying this strategy? What enterprise agility do you think Alibaba achieved in this phase?

4. From this case, we can easily find that Alibaba was changing its role along different phases. Because of that, the nature of the ecosystem changed as well. Can you conceptualize this change by drawing the structure of the ecosystem in each phase? Give a brief description of its evolution (with filled circle representing focal company, other un-filled geometric symbols representing members in the ecosystem).

Haier (1)

Miao Cui

Introduction

It was February 10, 2013 and also the Chinese New Year. Most employees at Haier Group (Haier) were enjoying the holiday and the Haier Industrial Park seemed extraordinarily empty. Mr. Zhou, the EVP and also the CMO of Haier, did not go for the vacation and was standing alone in front of his office windows. As one of the primary decision-makers, he had to figure out the next year's strategy of the electronic mall in a week. Should he reinforce the extant mass customization strategy or turn to the individual customization strategy? He had been wavering between the two options for almost two months. When this issue came to his mind, he could not help thinking about the development of Haier as well as the Chinese home appliance industry.

Haier's History

Haier, headquartered in Tsingtao, China, was founded in 1984 with imported refrigerator production technology from the German Liberhaier company (Haier, 2013). In the following three decades, Haier transformed from an insolvent small-sized firm to a world-leading white goods manufacturer and its global turnover got to RMB 163.1 billion (US$25.97 billion) in 2012. The company had established production facilities and R&D labs all over the world with about 80,000 employees and its products had served users in more than 100 countries and regions. Haier was ranked 8th in "the World's 50 Most Innovative Companies" by the Boston Consulting Group.

Haier was an enterprise filled with innovation genes. By the end of 2011, Haier who owned the most patents among the Chinese home appliance industry had applied for 12,318 patents, including 4,175 patents of invention. In addition, Haier paid close attention to management innovation and invented Overall Every Control and Clear (OEC), Individual-Goal Combination and many other management methods. Along with the innovation culture, Haier also believed in "Customers are always right," By holding the faiths, Haier gained customer recognition and experienced a rapid development.

Haier's development could be divided into 5 stages — brand building, diversifying, globalization, global branding and networking — which were aligned with its strategies (Figure 1).

Stage 1 (1984–1990): Brand Building

In the 1980s, while the Chinese home appliance market was still in short supply and many other companies rushed to increase production,

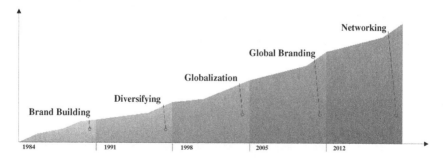

Figure 1. Haier's Development.

Haier did not blindly run after production but focused on improving product quality and implementing total quality management. One of the most famous stories about Haier was that Zhang Ruimin, the director at that time and the current CEO, took the lead in smashing 76 defective refrigerators. This made Haier famous for its production quality and gains a competitive advantage when the market was oversupplied.

Stage 2 (1991–1997): Diversifying

When the fierce completion led to the large-scale mergers and acquisitions (M&As), Haier, like other powerful enterprises, initiated M&As and implemented diversification strategy. To effectively activate and integrate the 18 acquired enterprises, Haier applied a kind of unique culture, activating shock fish culture, as Haier believed that the poor performance of those companies was on account of their lack of corporate culture, and that their performance would improve if proper culture was instilled. Meanwhile, at that time, the home appliance market was highly competitive and quality had become the basic needs of users. On realizing this, Haier not only implemented the total quality management, but also its "star service system". The superior and differentiated services enabled Haier to gain a competitive advantage during the price wars.

Stage 3 (1998–2004): Globalization

Since 1998, Haier changed its strategic focus and determined to run after globalization. Different with international goals of many other Chinese enterprises, Haier did not only run after globalization for foreign exchange, but more importantly, to create Haier's own brand. To fulfill the goals, Haier followed a three-step strategy, "going out, going into, and going up". They first entered into markets of developed countries to create a famous brand name and then entered into markets of developing countries by making use of the brand. In this stage, Haier gradually established its design, manufacturing, and marketing facilities and teams overseas.

Stage 4 (2005–2011): Global Branding

Haier upgraded the globalization strategy and implemented the global branding strategy since 2005. The rise and prevalence of e-commerce in China compelled manufacturers to pay more attention to user demands and enhanced users' central position. It drove Haier to change the direction of "Enterprises are the center and sell products to customers" into "Users are the center and Enterprises should sell services to customers". To accomplish the goals, Haier did not only leverage its own resources to serve users but also made use of resources scattered around the world, and integrated global R&D, manufacturing and marketing resources to create a global brand.

Stage 5 (2012–Present): Networking

On December 26, 2012, Haier announced the networking strategy to direct and encourage employees to fit into the e-commerce era. The strategy had two meanings: Building network-based or nodular marketing, logistics, and service systems to quickly and accurately meet customers' requirements and building nodular enterprise to break the corporate boundary and utilize superior resources beyond Haier.

Industry Background

Development of Chinese Home Appliance Industry

China's home appliance industry started in the early 1980s. Prior to that period, only a very small amount of Chinese families owned home appliances. The citizens' main concern was food and how to feed their families of four or more kids. This problem was particularly prominent in the 1950s and 1960s. It got improved in the 1970s, which could be told from the so-called "four pieces" of a wedding at that time, Shanghai brand watch, Flying Pigeon or Forever brand bicycle, radio set, and sewing machine. Following the Reform and Opening-up, the Chinese home appliance industry had been experiencing a rapid development in the last 30 years.

The first phase (1978–1990): Infancy phase

At this stage, the Chinese government strictly controlled the number of home appliance manufacturers; to establish a company, it was hard to get government permission. In 1978, the Chinese government approved the Shanghai TV factory's application to introduce the first color TV production line from Hitachi, Japan (Bai, 2008). Over the same period, Wanbao and Xiaoya introduced the first refrigerator and washing machine production line from Singapore and Italy in succession. In the following several years, Chinese home appliance manufacturers introduced foreign technologies to update their own outdated ones as well as to sustain in the changing market (Hu, 2008), e.g., color TV rather than black & white TV. The number of refrigerator manufacturers and washing machine manufacturers reached 70 and 80 respectively (Tencent, 2008). Despite the increasing number of manufacturers, home appliance products were in short supply and any purchase made at that time was accompanied by a certain commodity ticket.

The second phase (1991–1995): Rapid growth phase

In 1990, the Chinese government abolished the policy that only the designated enterprises were qualified to produce home appliance products and dozens of newly established home appliance manufacturers scattered around China. Many new brands emerged overnight. Although the supply shortage eased substantially, the market was still a seller's market. The relationship between the supply and demand resulted in an increase in prices of home appliance products and manufactures' profit margin was about 30%.

Meanwhile, Chinese home appliance manufacturers began to appear on the international stage. In 1992, 10 Chinese home appliance manufacturers participated in the Home Appliance & Household Consumables trade show held in Cologne, Germany. Also, the first Chinese international home appliance exhibition, the Beijing International Household Products & Technical Equipment Exhibition, was held in 1993. In addition, Chinese manufacturers began to export home appliance products overseas. For example, Qingdao Refrigerator Factory (Haier's predecessor) exported

90,000 refrigerators in 1992 and most of them were exported to Germany. Qingdao Refrigerator Factory became the largest Asian refrigerator exporter of the German market.

When the Chinese manufacturers got involved in international business transactions, multinational enterprises (MNEs) rushed into the Chinese market. MNEs were attracted by the rapid development and the prosperous future of the Chinese market. Simple technical investment was not able to meet MNEs' needs. Since 1994, many MNEs started to look for Chinese partners to set up international joint ventures. The German Company Bosch-Siemens Home Appliances Group co-invested with Xiaoya Group and set up BSW Household Appliances Co., Ltd. in December, 1994. And almost at the same time, American Whirlpool Corporation and Beijing Snowflake Electric Appliance Group Corporation established a joint venture, Beijing Whirlpool Snowflake Electrical Co., Ltd. By the end of 1994, multinational home appliance manufacturers had set up more than 20 joint ventures in China. The increasing number of home appliance manufacturers ensured the supply to the market which resulted in the reversal of the relation between the supply and demand. The Chinese market turned from a seller's market to a buyer's market.

The third phase (1996–Present): Mature phase

The increase in the number of home appliance manufacturers did not only transform the market, but also resulted in a fierce competition. In March, 1996, the Chinese Changhong Electronics Co., Ltd. (Changhong) announced a price cut and reduced the TV price by 8–18%. Two months later, the Chinese Konka Group followed the Changhong, and many other manufacturers also joined in the price war. The profit margin sharply decreased to 1–3%.

The price war made small and medium-sized manufacturers suffer. Many of them could not survive the price war. This led to a fierce buying spree. Konka Group, Kelong, Haier, and other large-sized enterprises established new production bases by merging small and medium-sized firms. This resulted in the formation of large-sized home appliance groups.

The price war did not end, though the industry centralization was improved. On the eve of the new millennium, some large-sized home appliance groups provoked another fierce price war. Hisense lowered its air conditioning product price in March. Notwithstanding, Haier, Gree, Kelong, and three other companies established an anti-price war alliance. The price war was rekindled when Kelong announced the cut in their air conditioning product price, which also led to a collapse of the alliance. The same thing happened in the TV and washing machine markets.

Since then, price wars have become commonplace in the Chinese home appliance market. These not only led to the second mergers and acquisitions wave, but also urged home appliance manufacturers to lower production cost in order to survive the competition. On one hand, Xiaoya, Xiamen Overseas Chinese Electronic Co., Ltd. (XOCECO), New Fly, Hualing, and other large-sized companies were merged with other stronger counterparts and the industry centralization was further improved, while on the other, to maintain certain profit margin in the fierce price competition, many manufacturers began to introduce information systems to facilitate process optimization and supply chain management. So far, all the large-sized home appliance manufacturers had established information systems.

Changes in Customer Demands

The rapid development of the Chinese home appliance industry transformed the Chinese market from a seller's market to a buyer's market, and customer demands changed over the years. In the seller's market phase, certain commodity tickets were required when buying home appliance products. Even though a buyer had enough money, he/she could not purchase a home appliance product without a ticket which was very scarce. In terms of price, prices of home appliance products remained the same over the years. Take the prices of refrigerators for example, the price of a medium-end refrigerator was RMB 2,000 in the late 1980s while the same level of product was sold at the same price in 2013. However, China's per capita income rose 8-fold in the past 20 years. Therefore, home appliance products were luxury goods for Chinese citizens in that period and people felt satisfied when they bought a home appliance product.

After the market transformation, consumers were not satisfied with buying a home appliance product any more. They paid more attention to price and quality. However, most manufacturers overemphasized on price. Only a few understood customer demands and placed more importance on quality.

As the industry became mature, customers required more than just a product and began to pay attention to services. Thus, they emphasized on home delivery and installation according to requirements and easy availability of maintenance and warranty services. This urged manufacturers to build service teams or develop service agents.

Development of Sales Channels

The development of the home appliance industry triggered the evolution of home appliance sales channels. In the 1980s, home appliance manufacturers relied on department stores to sell their products, since at that time for the Chinese, department stores were high-end business centers compared to frontage shops. Buyers at department stores rushed to factories to purchase home appliance products as it was a seller's market.

In the early 1990s, a new distribution channel, the home appliance product wholesale market, appeared and occupied a dominant position. These wholesalers were buyers at department stores originally who were familiar and built stable ties with home appliance manufacturers. These gave them priority to purchase home appliance products. Meanwhile, these buyers gradually built ties with dozens of sales terminals and developed their own sales networks, which in turn attracted manufacturers to sell products to wholesalers directly.

The wholesale markets were cleaned out at the end of 1994 as they exclusively relied on sales terminals to sell products and eliminate inventory, and eliminate inventory. This caused the inventory of the home appliance manufacturers was extremely high. Manufacturers could not recover money in a timely manner and some of them tried to switch to other channels. In addition, manufacturers also directly supplied products to large-sized supermarkets. Some innovative manufacturers began to establish direct stores.

Observing the huge demands on sales agents, some powerful and farsighted companies and individuals invested in establishing home appliance chain enterprises since 1995. Gome, Suning, and other retail chain enterprises were set up at that time. Compared to establishing and operating direct stores, costs were extremely low for home appliance manufacturers to sell products through chain stores around China. In addition, home appliance chain stores were welcomed by the Chinese as prices were relatively low than those sold in department stores and direct stores, thereby chain stores quickly occupied half of the Chinese market share. The success of the retail chain enterprises rendered them advantageous over the manufacturers. This could be told from the battle between Gree and Gome in 2004. On February 17, 2004, Gome announced it would initiate the "Air Conditioning War Plan," and executed the plan three days later. Noticing this, Gree asked Gome to restore the prices of its products but was rejected. Thereafter, Gree stopped supply of products to Gome; in retaliation, Gome withdrew Gree's products nationwide.

Haier: Changes in Organizational Structure and Development of Information System

Haier's organizational structure was always in the adjustment. Big adjustment happened once or twice a year, let alone small adjustments. Zhang Ruimin believed:

> "Every enterprise should establish an ordered but non-equilibrium structure. The ordered and equilibrium structure is a stable structure and lacks energy and the disordered and non-equilibrium structure is doomed to chaotic. Haier devotes to create a new equilibrium when it is non-equilibrium and break equilibrium when it is equilibrium."

Haier's organizational structure mainly experienced changes from linear functional to matrix, to market chain and to nodular organizational structure. The last two were supported by the information system (IS) development.

Linear Functional Organizational Structure

Haier adopted the linear functional organizational structure (Figure 2) since establishment. During that period, the subordinate enterprises have to listen to the group's command in terms of corporate culture, personnel deployment, project investment, financial budget and final accounts, technology development, quality certification and management, marketing, and services. This structure worked quite well until 1991 when the quality of employees was very low and the internal management was chaotic and only by adopting the linear functional organizational structure, Haier could effectively control the employees and stabilize production.

Matrix Organization Structure

In 1991, when beginning to launch M&As and implement the diversification strategy, Haier found out that the linear functional organizational structure was not suitable any more. Haier's large enterprise disease was gradually revealed at that time, i.e., slow response and resource waste. To improve the response capacity and avoid duplication of efforts, Haier turned to the matrix organizational structure (Figure 3). There were two

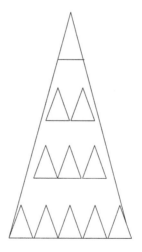

Figure 2. The Linear Functional Structure.

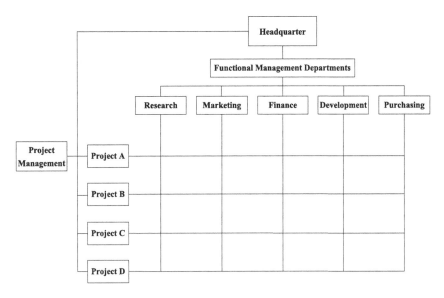

Figure 3. The Matrix Structure.

coordinate axes: The abscissa axis was defined as divisions, e.g., refrigerator, washing machine, air conditioning division; and the vertical axis was defined as functional departments, e.g., finance, human resources, and R&D department. The adjusted structure changed Haier's focus from functions to projects and facilitated the company to carry out and promote multiple projects simultaneously.

Market Chain Organizational Structure and IS Development

In 1998, Haier began to explore the market chain organizational structure (Figure 4) after finding disadvantages of the matrix organizational structure, e.g., multiple leadership and competition for resources. Market chain referred to introducing the market interest adjustment mechanism into enterprise internal management, changing the original administrative feature of business relationship between up-and-down processes and positions into the equal trading, service, and contractual relationship, converting external order forms into a series of internal order forms. To forge the

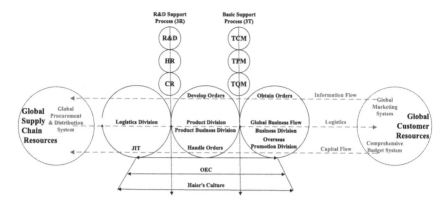

Figure 4.   The Market Chain Structure.

market chain, Haier conducted a great degree of adjustment on its original divisions: Integrated manufacture systems scattering in different divisions into product business division; integrated R&D resources into product division; separated financial, procurement and sales departments from each division and integrated into the capital, logistics, and business promotion division; integrated other departments and formed innovative order-support divisions, 3R (R&D, HR, and CR), and basic order fulfillment support divisions, 3T (TCM, TPM, and TQM). The activities of production, logistics, and capital divisions consisted of the main processes of the market chain, while the 3R and 3T activities consisted of the auxiliary processes. Marketing, procurement, and settlement were unifiedly controlled and carried out by the Group, and the 3R and 3T registered as independent business service companies. In addition, Haier's culture and its OEC management system laid the foundation for the implementation of the market chain.

In the new process, the business promotion division was responsible for building the global marketing network and obtaining orders from customers around the world. This mode effectively decreased the marketing cost as marketing teams could market various kinds of products simultaneously. Meanwhile, it also benefitted customers who would not have to discuss cooperation respectively with the TV, washing machine, refrigerator, and other marketing teams. The logistics promotion division was responsible for building Haier's global procurement and distribution network by using global supply chain resources. The establishment and operation of the logistics promotion division helped Haier to obtain high-quality parts, reduce inventory, and improve cash flow rate as the division devoted to Just-In-Time (JIT) procurement and distribution of raw materials and products. The establishment of the capital promotion division was aimed at solving the high bad debts caused by the original trade mode in which individual divisions directly exchanged with banks, suppliers, and customers and to realize spot cash and zero bad debts. The product division, supported by the 3R processes, was responsible for meeting customer demands by developing new products and market researches while the product business division, supported by the 3T processes, produced products according to orders.

The successful fulfillment of the market chain depended largely on the building and Haier's IS building and continuous improvement. As Haier's CEO recalled:

"At that time, I strongly believed that the IS project would help Haier to create a new management system."

Actually, it was in 1997 that Haier began to develop the IS. At that time, Haier's focus was to realize basic applications and build the backbone network and basic office applications, covering sales companies and call centers. When Zhang Ruimin announced the initiation of the market chain transformation, Haier accelerated the construction of IS and developed a complete order information-centered IS, which mainly included:

- An e-commerce platform. In 2000 Haier developed the first B2C e-commerce platform, with payment function, in China.
- A B2B trading platform. Haier established a B2B trading platform to support online procurement.
- An integrated synchronous supply chain management platform. The platform connected and ran through logistics, sales, production, purchasing, warehousing, and financial and cost management.
- Manufacturing Execution System (MES). MES facilitated Haier to track and control production quality.

- A one-stop customer service system. From 1998–2005, Haier built a centralized customer service management system in four phases respectively, including call centers across the country, more than 30,000 service outlets and 42 spare parts management centers scattered around the country.

Haier did not feel satisfied with the performance of market chain. To further strengthen its effect, in 2005, Haier advocated the "Integrating Order with Personnel" management mode, in which personnel referred to every employee in Haier and order referred to competitive market targets. "Integrating Order with Personnel" required every employee to act as an innovative individual and a strategic business unit (SBU), and be capable of hitting competitive market targets. The underlying principle was that only by occupying and using resources could employees finish orders and create new value for Haier.

To calculate purchase, sale, cost, value-added and loss of every employee created for each order, Haier further improved its IS. The main improvement was to add electronic profit and loss account function into the existing IS based on the market chain processes. By applying this function, Haier could obtain every employee's daily cost and value, thereby facilitating the implementation of the market chain mode.

Although the market chain mode helped Haier to improve its performance, there were still some shortcomings, which hindered Haier from achieving high goals. An SBU was relatively independent and lacked cooperation. Often, to complete one's own order and achieve high performance, an SBU might harm the interests of other SBUs. To solve the problem, in 2007, Haier further announced and transformed SBUs to self-operated entities (SOEs). Different from SBUs, SOEs were connected by contracts and it was obvious who was responsible for losses. The common denominator of SBUs and SOEs was that both of them were self-operated and self-financing. There were three types of SOEs, R&D, manufacture, and market. SOEs were nested. The smallest SOE could be an employee of him or herself. A larger one could be Tsingtao community store SOE which included 80 stores, or three door refrigerator SOE consisting of several R&D, manufacture, and marketing SOEs, but the largest SOE was Haier itself.

Nodular Organizational Structure

In 2012, Haier innovated the organizational structure again. Since then, SOEs were transformed to community of interests (COI) and Haier changed into a nodular organization (Figure 5). It was worthy of note that the organizational restructuring of this time was different from those before as it did not only involve internal organizational structure changes but also involved external stakeholders which forged Haier as a boundless resource network.

When asked why Haier was determined to transform to a boundless nodular organization, Mr. Gong, the head of the electronic mall strategy department described the reason as:

"In 2011, home appliance online shopping became prevalent in China. Haier began to co-operate with 360Buy, T-mall, and other e-commerce businesses in a timely manner to sell home appliance products online. And we also established our own electronic mall in 2012. Following the online sale, we noticed that we could access large amount of customers' feedback and demand information as customers were willing to pen down their comments. This led us to know that customer demands are diversified and fast-changing. The existing modes, no matter the R&D, manufacture, marketing, service, inventory management or logistics, could not meet

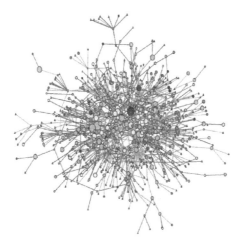

Figure 5. The Nodular Structure

customers' requirement. To cope with the networked market, we should transform into a nodular enterprise."

Mr. Wang, the liaison between service and e-commerce department and also a member of the service department, further gave an example to illustrate the necessity of the restructuring.

"Haier engaged in an online promotion activity during the last Mother's Day ... A customer asked Haier to deliver a bunch of flowers with the refrigerator he purchased. To be honest, we would not be able to do it with the market chain structure as the information would be conveyed from the market SOE to the manufacture SOE and to the logistics SOE and manufacture SOE could not deal with the information of sending flowers. However, we can achieve it with the nodular structure as the customer's demand information was conveyed to the manufacture division and service division simultaneously."

Actually, the nodularity strategy laid a solid foundation for the restructuring. In recent years, Haier's white goods division had been committing to nodularity and achieved the goal from every process, including design, research, manufacture, and marketing.

Haier's network consisted of countless nodes and relations between the nodes. The nodes comprised several individuals. And the number of individuals depended on the per capita income maximization principle, i.e., any new members were asked to contribute to his/her team's performance and the contribution should be greater than the previous per capita income, or his/her unique value. When talking to the team building mechanism, Mr. Wang explained that:

"If a potential new member can provide unique value to our customers, of course, I will invite him/her in. Similarly, if any existing member's contribution is limited or harmful to our average performance, we will surely expel him/her from our team. The reason for the practice is very simple. Any newly added member will share our profit and we will have to pay for the cost of adding him/her. No one is willing to work with valueless members."

In addition, teams or so-called nodes were dynamic. They assembled and separated according to orders. When there was a new order, several new teams would be built to complete the order. And when the order was finished, these teams would be disbanded and members had to look for position in a new team.

In addition, relations between the nodes were dynamic. These nodes were assembled and separated according to orders as well. When there was a new order, several nodes would assemble as a COI. Different from SOEs, contracts signed among nodes in a COI were user-centered. This mechanism effectively avoided gaming between SOEs. Mr. Zou, the head of white goods supply chain department, explained the reason as follows:

"Before, contracts were signed with upstream and downstream sectors. To assure the safety of their own interests, an SOE might harm others' interests. Take a market SOE for example, to increase sales, this SOE might sign low-end product sales contracts with customers and required R&D SOEs to design and development the low-end products. Compared with R&D high-end products, the R&D of low-end products hardly contributed to the profit and loss account of the R&D SOEs. After transforming into COIs, any COI is asked to establish a benchmark, i.e., a goal of being the leader in the industry, and every SOE taking part in the COI will sign a customer-centered contract to specify its responsibility and resources needed. By applying this contract, it was clear for every SOE what users needed, what other SOEs required and what its responsibility was. To achieve these goals, R&D personnel and market personnel always carry out market research together."

To better realize the cooperation between nodes, Haier also set a position called liaison within each node. Liaisons were responsible for coordinating cooperation between nodes. Mr. Wang illustrated his job as follows:

"To be honest, I assume myself as a member of e-commerce department rather than service department though I work for the latter. My job is to provide high quality services to e-commerce department. Whatever they ask for, I try my best to meet their requirements. This is the way I create value and earn salaries. If they have any demand for service, it's fine for them to list the demands and come to me. That's all! If in the past, they would have to visit 10 or more person to discuss the services."

Actually, the liaisons were also dynamic rather than changeless and only those who were able to achieve high performance and stakeholder satisfaction, and access high-quality resources for their team could stay on the position. Otherwise, the liaison would be substituted by other more qualified individuals.

In addition to the internal structure, Haier also broke the organizational boundary, and dynamically cooperated with a large amount of individuals and organizations outside. Those outsiders became the main innovators for Haier to meet users' requirements in a timely fashion. When recognizing customer needs, Haier would post the information on its R&D platform, which could be seen by professional design and technology consultant companies. Or Haier would directly contact companies with strong capabilities.

To locate these powerful suppliers, in 2012, Haier carried out the supplier selection and refinement project. The supplier chain division was required to figure out the Top 10 products of each category, suppliers of each module, the advantages and disadvantages of each module as well as the corresponding customer demands. By this project, Haier established a supplier database to facilitate the company to look for proper module.

Sometimes, assurance of single module quality was not enough and the most important thing was to obtain a high-quality system. To achieve the goal by accessing external technologies, Haier designed the external supplier collaboration mechanism. Mr. Zou illustrated it as follows:

"Take the refrigerator intelligent system design project for example. To provide the best products to users, we got together the relevant companies and told them we wanted a high-quality system not modules. Then these companies combined freely and formed a COI. Finally, we chose the best system and of course its suppliers. The result was quite different from what we could get before. In the past, we only required best modules and assemble them by ourselves. It was not able to ensure that we could design and produce best systems ... what we need to do is to recognize and understand customer demand and figure out which suppliers can meet the demands."

The match job, matching customer demands with external partners' supply, was achieved by liaisons. A liaison described his role switch as follows:

"I worked for the e-commerce department. Before, I was an R&D engineer and now I'm a liaison. My major job is to look for proper suppliers who can meet customer demands."

Similar with liaisons between departments, liaisons between Haier and suppliers were dynamic. Only those who were able to access high-quality resources could stay on the position.

To accomplish the dramatic restructuring, Haier committed a lot. As the head of the process, system and innovation (PSI) department, he quoted that:

"The biggest challenge for the restructuring is process and information system."

Both the restructuring and process changes needed the support of IS adjustment. To facilitate the operation of the electronic mall and restructuring, Haier further improved the IS. On one hand, Haier developed two new subsystems, the order acceptance system and the order distribution system, to deal with online orders, and also redeveloped the website and community platforms to collect customer demands. To use these data efficiently, Haier also developed some data mining tools to refine customer demand information.

On the other hand, Haier carried out a lot of work to open up subsystems. The prototype of Haier's IS was SAP's ERP which was a linear system, and data were transmitted from upstream to downstream. However, the nodular organization needed a networked system, which could realize the real-time transmission. To achieve the goal, Haier opened up the original subsystems, including product life cycle management system (PLM), supply chain management system (SCM), customer relation management system (CRM), Go-to-Market system and other subsystems. By opening up these subsystems, Haier was able to speed up data transmission, synchronize data in five minutes and fulfill it within 24-hour delivery promise to users.

Looking Ahead

Haier was able to provide mass customization TV products to users through years of effort. "Users can choose the functions they want, such as 3D function and internet function, and only pay for the functions they choose, which is quite different from before." Mrs. Wang, a leading official of brand marketing sector illustrated the mass customization.

Mr. Zhou smiled when he thought of Haier's achievement of mass customization. However, he had no idea what to do next. There were two options.

- To implement the individual customization strategy in the TV business immediately. Haier was a synonym of innovator and was always on the leading position in the industry. Individual customization was an inevitable development trend of the industry. And the one who could realize individual customization first in the industry was doomed to occupy an advantageous position. However, this might put too much burden on Haier's IS as more qualitative changes were needed and costs were always very high. Should Haier pre-actively try to implement individual customization strategy?
- To expand the mass customization strategy to other businesses. Although realizing mass customization in the TV business, other business areas had not kicked the goal. In terms of other products, the standardization of modules had not achieved the sufficient level. If Haier chose to expand the mass customization strategy to other businesses first, notwithstanding, the IS was needed for improvement, it would be a kind of quantitative changes rather than qualitative changes. Haier was capable to cope with it. Therefore, it might be more reasonable for Haier to expand the mass customization strategy to other businesses first.

Mr. Zhou still hesitated on what to do next? Whether to implement the individual customization strategy in the TV business immediately or to expand the mass customization strategy to other businesses, he had no idea.

References

Bai, Y.M. *Mitsui Empire in the Action*: *Uncover the Layout Manager of the Nippon Foundation*, China Economic Publishing House, Beijing, 2008.
Haier. 2013. Haier Group Profile. http://www.haier.net/cn/about_haier/, 3 May 2013.
Hu, Y. 2008. *Haier Reaches Higher*. Hangzhou: Zhengjiang People's Publishing House.
Tencent. 2008. 30 Years of Reform and Opening up: The Development of the Chinese Home Appliance Industry. http://cq.qq.com/a/20081008/000228.htm, 3 May 2013.

Discussion Questions

1. Why did Haier implement the mass customization strategy?
2. How did Haier achieve flexibility?
3. How did Haier's IS contribute to flexibility?
4. If you were Mr. Zhou, which strategy would you agree on? Why?

Haier (2)

Zheng Wang and Taohua Ouyang

*"The most impressive experience of working at Haier is that we made a
big leap from playing a supporting role to being a strategic decision-maker
over the past 15 years."*

— CIO of Haier

Background

On March 27, 2009, the "Haier Hammer" had been collected by the
National Museum of China as a national relic. This hammer was used by
the CEO of Haier, Ruimin Zhang, in 1985 to smash 76 newly produced
refrigerators that were found to have serious defects. His radical action
tremendously aroused the workers' and managers' awareness of product
quality. Haier Group started as the Qingdao Refrigerator Plant in the early
1980s and nearly filed for bankruptcy after a few years of establishment due
to deficit financing of up to RMB 1,470,000 (US$230,000). In 1984, the
current CEO of Haier, Ruimin Zhang, took over the company and began to
make fundamental management changes at Haier, especially focusing on
quality control. From then on, Haier Group has gradually established itself
as a world-renowned brand with excellent quality and services. Today,
Haier Group is the world's 4th largest manufacturer of white goods and one

of China's top 100 IT companies. By 2010, the 26-year-old Haier had successfully built its production and sales network to include 30 overseas factories and manufacturing bases, 18 research and development centers, 10 industrial parks, 58,800 sales offices and 96 product group categories, ranging from refrigerators and washing machines to computers and televisions. It currently has more than 50,000 employees worldwide and has achieved an annual revenue of US$20.7 billion for the year 2010.

During the 27-year developmental journey of Haier, strategic transformation and business process reengineering (BPR) have been constantly promoted within Haier to enhance its operations, responding speedily to market and services. The backbone of supporting these changes undoubtedly rely on the high-end information systems that Haier adopted, which include enterprise resource planning (ERP) systems, procurement systems, B2B and B2C websites and customer relationship management (CRM) systems. After full utilization of these systems, the responding time to orders has been reduced to 10 days from 36 days on average. The Just-In-Time (JIT) mode has been achieved in procurement and delivery services, reducing the rate of the slack products by 73% and the area of warehouse by 50%. Meanwhile, the earning capacity of the logistic center has been improved by 40 times. Capital turnover has been reduced to 10 days and the procurement cycle has been reduced to 3 days. However, Rome cannot be built in one day. The outstanding achievements of Haier's informatization that we see today experienced a 15-year long journey since the first day when the IT (Information Technology) department was established in 1994.

Overview — The Development of IT Department

In the wake of Haier's strategic transformation (i.e., build nation-wide brand) and change of organizational structure in the middle of the 1990s, the IT department was established, which placed Haier in the first group of enterprises in China to invest in emerging IT. A manager of IT division one noted:

> "In the period of 1995 to 1997, Haier aimed to build a nation-wide famous brand. So, we made great expansion on our production line, sales network and customer services. IT was the backbone that supported all this vision."

From then on, Haier subsequently invested large amounts of funds and human resources for improving Haier's IT capabilities. At the initial developmental phase (1994–1997), the establishment of official corporate websites (www.haier.com) and replacement of computers offered Haier a number of opportunities to not only promote itself and its products on an international scale but also provide a platform for having contacts with potential overseas collaborators in terms of trading negotiation, product ordering, and customer services, all of which formed a solid foundation for Haier's informatization strategy. At the growing phase (1998–2004), the IT department of Haier aimed to digitize its procurement systems and supply chain systems so as to catch up with the pace of Haier's fast expansions. Meanwhile, the IT department linked up the information flow among departments at Haier by leveraging multiple systems that put it in place. However, the maximum value of these systems has not been fully realized yet. At the mature phase (2005–Present), the IT department is currently integrating and maintaining the isolated systems across the organization in order to provide product supplies and inventories on a global scale. On June 1, 2008, the IT department of Haier successfully built its first "Global Value System" operating platform, which provides vigorous supports for 84 business processes, 129 legal persons, and 42 industrial and trading companies worldwide. The platform has been historically ranked as the largest ERP-based systems, which involve the most legal persons and the most complicated business processes in the history of SAP's implementation in the global context.

Over the 15-year development, the IT department has shifted gradually from a supporting function to a strategic decision-maker, as the manager of the IT strategy division commented:

"We felt that the jobs we do today are very different from those in old days when the IT department was just established. We are currently playing a much more critical role to the group than before. "

The number of employees in the IT department increased from 10 people at its creation to 265 people today. Next, three important developmental phases will be described in detail.

Phase 1: Automation (1994–1997)

"The top management of Haier keeps on encouraging employees at IT department to set higher target to revolutionize Haier's information systems."

— Manager of IT strategy division

Building the informatization foundation

With the booming Chinese economy and the worldwide new trend of IT development in the mid-1990s, Haier's top management had a vision of leveraging the novel IT to strengthen its existing business operations. As a senior IT research executive noted:

"Haier tried to pursue new high on its business development through establishment of 4 more factories in 1997, making the total number of agent company selling Haier's products up to 42. So, there was an urgent need of managing the complicated business operations through leveraging on IT."

With this vision in mind, Haier invested more than US$4.5 million to introduce new technologies into the organization in an effort to replace manual work with computer-based work. The need of inputting technologies was further triggered by Haier's new strategy of creating famous brands in China. Specifically, the introduced information technologies were primarily focused on improving two aspects of Haier's businesses namely, organizational image and business operation.

- **Building positive organizational image.** Haier's IT department cooperated closely with an external vendor to build its first official corporate website. The manager of IT division three noted as follows:

"While Haier started to expand its business scale, the pressures on the IT department were very intense. We must be responsible for achieving the organization's vision by bringing refreshing IT capabilities into Haier and the driving the learning efforts."

The website not only helped Haier to rapidly market its products and organization, and enabled it to have business footprints worldwide, but also served as an information-gathering center for Haier headquarters and its subsidiaries across China. In 1997, based on the positive feedback received from the website endeavor, the IT department was authorized to build Haier's customer service center and call center to form a network of service information that was available nationwide. Upon its completion, Haier was able to provide information services to more than 7,000 customers per day and thus gained a reputation for excellent customer service. In the words of the manager of the IT division three,

"To respond the impetus from top management, we aimed to build the intranet and official website in 1996 and were among the first batch of enterprise in China who owned customer service centre via phone in 1997."

- **Revolutionizing business operation.** To replace manual work, Haier had introduced a number of new technologies including CAD/CAM/CAE systems, computers, automation systems, etc. The manager of IT division one noted:

"By cooperating with external vendor, IT department was able to bring refreshing solutions to Haier's problems, thereby driving Haier's IT changes rapidly."

To reap a positive outcome out of these initiatives, the IT department was undoubtedly ordered to take the lead of the system implementations so as to keep an eye on the progress of both the system building and use, because these changes were fundamental and radical, which requires an appropriate way to manage. The manager of strategy division reflected on their efforts in revolutionizing business operation with new technologies:

"The application of CAD that led by IT department shortened the development cycles of IT systems, thereby transforming customers' potential need into actual products in a swift manner. Meeting the market need faster improved the company's competitive edge tremendously."

Assimilating the new changes

Nevertheless, such fundamental change affected Haier's operations to some extent because most of employees had to spend some time to assimilate the new technologies both inside and outside of the IT department rather than focus on their current work, thereby significantly deferred the positive effect of these new technologies that should be brought into Haier, as confirmed by the manager of IT division one:

> "In responding the urgency of facilitating Haier's new strategy vision and China's IT development, we introduced a number of technologies to our business operation, including office automation and accounting computerization. It was very challenging initially as we lacked qualified employees to use the systems, but they understood that the IT change is necessary and getting used to the new way of doing things is a must."

Initially, IT department was also at a loss with the radical IT-related organizational change, leading to the minimum support that they can provide for the employees. As a senior IT researcher noted:

> "Since the firm expanded so rapidly, many problems started to emerge, including requirement of just-in-time service, inaccurate product delivery and drop of customer satisfaction. We as an IT department did not know how to help with."

However, with the instructive orders from the top managements and the urgency feeling of completing the tasks given inside of the IT department, an effective plan was worked out. To solve the issues of computer operations that most employees encountered, the IT department recruited external experts to train its IT staff in the implemented technologies. After the IT staff had fully mastered these technologies, one-on-one training was provided to the rest of the Haier staff who might potentially need to use the technologies. In the words of the manager of IT division one:

> "We did not provide formal training. All of our training was provided on a one to one basis. Employees from IT department taught other system users step by step. We would not stop training them until they were able to use the system to receive orders and distribute jobs."

On one hand, as the training was provided, employees started to realize that the new system can help with reducing their workload tremendously. For example, the inventory administrator used to make records manually. With the increasing number of product categories and quantities, they found it was easy to make mistakes. After mastering the new systems introduced, they noticed that the information systems could help with working efficiency and gradually took the initiatives to learn more about the system. On the other hand, to drive the technological change introduced in Haier, top management introduced a policy stating that staff would be qualified to work only after receiving a training certificate from the IT department, as commented by the manager of IT infrastructure division:

> "For the new system implemented in Haier, top management urgently wanted to see the return out of it, so a number of policies were constituted to diver employees' initiatives of learning in a swift manner."

Before information systems were introduced, employees who are outside of the IT department did not have the concept of so-called "processes" and they only understood their own responsibility. When IT employees started to train other employees for the new systems, the first thing they would understand was the processes they got involved. Gradually, employees understood the value of their work and relationship with the downstream and upstream of the process. More importantly, they knew how to bring advantage to the overall process through their own hands. The IT department had normalized employees' daily working routines and had drove employees' initiatives to a large extent. As a senior IT research executive noted:

> "With the expansion, the traditional way of paper-based working practice was unable to handle such large amount of information simultaneously. We were then trying to fulfill what has been asked from the top management."

Haier's initial IT-related efforts served as a starting point for its informatization. Although Haier's first IT attempt yielded some benefits at the operational level (such as shortening the product research period), its IT vision in that period was not fully realized. The manager of IT division two noted:

> "Haier's IT development was consistent with the overall trend of Chinese IT development. Although we established our IT department in 1995, it

only provided basic supporting function to some minor business, such as procurement of IT hardware."

Phase 2: Input of Multiple Systems (1998–2004)

"Comparing with period of 1994 to 1997, the biggest change we made in phase two was to integrate the isolated systems across Haier so as to provide visualized data for the entire business process, reflecting the "end to end" visualization required by the top management."

— Manager of IT division one

Inefficiency of information processing

Before 1998, a product-oriented organizational structure governed by IT-enabled automation enabled Haier to rapidly diversify its product offerings. Although the rapid expansion exceeded Haier's capability to handle information in 1998, the benefits brought by increased IT capabilities were diluted by the excessive coordination efforts between different product departments due to the emergence of boundaries. A senior IT researcher noted:

"From September 1998, Haier started to make transformations on business processes. To facilitate these efforts, since each product department had its own IT division who was working on promoting learning new IT knowledge previously, now we were connecting these divisions together to build a unified platform for each process."

Incomplete and inefficient information flow within the organization would inevitably put Haier in a risky situation in which its current business model, including marketing, logistics and finance, was seriously affected by the new, fast-paced market conditions, forming barriers to Haier's vision of becoming an internationally recognized brand at its second phase. Therefore, the CEO brought out an idea of solving the "time" and "space" problems via "speed". The main idea behind this was to improve operational agility through integrated business processes. With the request from the top management, the main focus of IT staffs' jobs was then on how to help the organization to respond to the market in a fast manner. In the words of manager of IT division two:

> *"As our businesses expanded in 1998, such as establishment of many overseas factories and research centers, the most important thing we faced was how to shorten the information flow cycles across the globe so that respond to the market faster."*

Fulfillment of multiple systems

From 1998 to 2004, in order to respond to the market in a speedy and flexible manner, Haier reengineered its business processes by unifying marketing, procurement, and finance across all product departments, as commented by the manager of IT division three:

> *"With the business process reengineering started, we felt that although employees were placed in the same department for the purpose of integrating business processes, the IT knowledge within them were still isolated. We as IT department felt we should focus on spanning IT knowledge boundaries rather than keeping on bringing up new systems without well-prepared."*

In addition, Haier aimed to increase its market shares worldwide and started to establish factories and research centers overseas. To fulfill these two needs, the IT department introduced a number of information systems in the following years.

The manager of strategy division commented the system initiatives at Haier:

> *"Prior to the inputs of these systems, we thought a project should be completely finished as long as its implementation was done. But now we have to watch all the way through its implementation and use till we found it is fully effective."*

Although a series of systems were input into Haier's operation, each information system was built for its own purpose without taking an overall consideration on its use for the whole business process. Therefore, IT department must integrate the isolated systems together so as to span the boundary within the business process. In the wake of the IT department's efforts, Haier was able to outperform its competitors in terms of responding to the market in a swift manner, as confirmed by the manager of IT division one:

"With the strategic shift from business expansion to fast responding to market, we realized that we have to integrate current business processes so as to better exert its own performance."

The IT department consolidated Haier's IT infrastructure by unifying marketing, logistics and finance procedures based on the solid IT knowledge built across Haier in the first phase. Given the efforts, employees are getting used to link up the IT knowledge to have a holistic picture of the organizational operations. The manager of IT division four noted:

"After 1998, when Haier proposes some new management ideas, IT department has to fulfill the needs based on prior IT knowledge and have close corporation with external vendor to link up the processes across departments."

For example, prior to the unification of logistics procedures, each product department had to make its own procurements from a number of different vendors. By leveraging BBP systems, the procurement procedure was standardized for all of the product departments and was restricted to purchases from only two regular vendors, which significantly reduced the procurement costs. As commented by the manager of IT division two:

"Taking procurement as an example, prior to introduction of ERP, the process was very complicated and time-consuming. With the long time promotion of IT department on the ERP systems, Haier grasped the essence of ERP systems and divided the procurement into three divisions: one for supply-seeking, one for bargaining price and signing contracts and one for stock taking."

Based on the IT foundation built previously, the IT department transformed Haier's IT knowledge from basic IT use to a higher level of IT-based business process standardization, reducing the necessary coordination efforts through spanning boundaries that blocked information flows between product departments, as commented by a senior IT researcher:

"During 1998 to 2004, information systems covered nearly every single department at Haier and maintained close information sharing among departments."

At the end of phase two, the top management was able to visualize the entire business process to find out which part of the process is being affected by the information log in a quick manner, thereby leading to fast response to the market as a whole. In the words of the manager of division two:

"We aimed to provide the top management with visualized data by penetrating deeply into each business process and put together all the information as a whole."

Phase 3: Ubiquitous Integration of Systems (2005–Present)

"Since from 2005, we have been working on integrating the information systems onto a same platform from where every participant is able to grasp information directly. The platform will gradually evolve IT employees' routines, from spanning boundaries to being a major player."

— Manager of IT division three

Shift of strategic direction

Before 2005, IT department was under strategy department so they were named IT strategy department. In order to promote innovation further, IT department was spun off from strategy department and IT department now is called process and system innovation department. The spin-off was severed as a prerequisite for Haier's new strategy. Although Haier entered the strategic phase of developing a globalized brand in 2005, the backend systems could not keep up the pace necessary to support this vision. The manager of strategy division revealed:

> *"The strategy had been shifted from internationalization to globalization. These two sounds very similar but there is a difference. Internationalization focuses only on the market perspective, but globalization needs more considerations on the service rather than only the market. However, our systems are not ready for this vision yet."*

Two major problems from previous phases have yet to be solved. First, the systems implemented in phase two were not fully utilized, resulting in resource wasting and information distortion, as a senior IT researcher noted:

> *"Each IT division worked for their own product department, regardless of what was currently happening at the organizational level."*

Second, the IT department adopted a learning-by-doing approach to build Haier's information systems and lacked a thoughtful plan for the implementation as a whole. A senior IT research executive noted:

> *"We were not clear about how we could help with the new strategy until 2007."*

In 2007, aiming to solve these problems, the CEO of Haier proposed the idea of an "information revolution" that would last for 1,000 days. Therefore, the major responsibility of the IT department in phase three is to integrate all 600 isolated systems and to make efforts to establish connections with overseas factories to fulfill the need for configuring resources in a global context. In addition to this responsibility, the CEO of Haier proposed an "order fulfillment system for every single employee", which means that every employee at Haier must make his or her own prediction about how many products he or she must produce or sell in a day, a week and a month, as commented by the manager of strategy division:

> *"Our group aims to set sell targets for every single employee within the group. What have been supporting this vision are also the information systems."*

The manager of IT division three added:

> *"The basic idea behind the ordering fulfillment system is to set individual targets for every employee within Haier and the ordering fulfillment system can be used as a monitoring tool to achieve this goal."*

This proposal put much pressure on the IT department, which was required to lead the process. Once the system is successfully implemented, it will be the backbone of Haier's entire operation. Therefore, the IT department must be able to drive the fulfillment of the vision.

Missions of IT department

From 2005 to the present, the IT department has focused primarily on two missions. One is to build the order fulfillment system and operationalize its use; the other is to build the so-called "Global Value Systems" that are centered around the ERP system and involve many other systems, as commented by the manager of strategy division:

> *"With the support of our Global Value Systems, our group is able to respond to the market in a swift and clear manner by providing localized production, design and marketing worldwide."*

The achievements of these two missions are vital for the survival of Haier in the global context. In order to meet Haier's globalized brand vision, the IT department is making ongoing efforts to explore the values of the developed systems to create a better fit with its strategic target, and it has become involved in many decision-making processes, as noted by a senior IT research executive:

> *"Even though each IT division had done their bests to fulfill the strategic need, but the cumulative efforts did not pay off immediately. So we need to have a long-term development strategy in mind."*

When the CEO proposed the "1000-day information revolution" in 2007, the CIO was the core decision maker in the boardroom, which indicates that IT department has been transformed from its initial supporting function to that of a strategic decision maker, as noted by the CIO:

> *"IT department takes the major reasonability of leading the 1000-day information revolution and is the decision maker on business process changes within the organization to fulfill the ordering fulfillment system vision from top management."*

Ongoing Efforts of IT Department

Over the 15-year development, IT department of Haier today has been playing a much more critical role than it was at its creation. The overall development of Haier discloses that today's enterprises must rely on high-end information systems to be able to respond to the market in a fast manner, which has been considered as an important business imperative in the dynamic environment. In the growth path of Haier, the role of IT department has been evolving over time to enable Haier responding to the markets and business opportunities swiftly. Such evolving role is still ongoing... In the words of the current CIO of Haier:

> *"The systems that we implemented today are actually aimed for two purposes. One is to support our business process, which has been achieved very well. The other is to support our strategic process. The latter one is still at its beginning stage. Although we put the Global Value Systems in place, the work we have been busy with is to make the GVS working for our strategic process, such as the process of our 'order fulfillment strategy'."*

The ultimate goal of Haier's IT department is to constantly strive for achieving higher targets so as to be an indispensable decision maker in the boardroom of top management.

Discussion Questions

1. In your opinion, what is IT organizational identity? How is it different from organizational identity and workgroup identity?
2. Why is it important for Haier to build and maintain appropriate IT organizational identity at different time?
3. What factors have triggered the need of IT organizational identity recreation at Haier? What are the steps to recreate IT organizational identity?
4. How do you classify the different types of IT organizational identities created in Haier's case?

China Mobile

Barney Tan and Carmen Mei Ling Leong

Organization and Project Background

China Mobile was incorporated on April 20, 2000 and is currently the world's largest mobile telecommunications provider in terms of network size, number of customers, and market value. Listed on both the Hong Kong and New York stock exchanges, China Mobile currently holds assets in excess of US$135 billion and ranks 77th in the Fortune Global 500 list (*Fortune Magazine* 2010). With the State-Owned Asset Supervision and Administration Commission (SASAC) of the Chinese Government as its largest shareholder, China Mobile has established an extensive network of subsidiaries in 31 provinces, autonomous regions, and directly administered municipalities across China and currently commands a 70.6% market share in the domestic telecommunications market. It has an estimated 150,000 employees and serves a customer base of over 600 million worldwide.

China Mobile's environmental sustainability initiative was formalized as one of five major programs of a new Corporate Social Responsibility (CSR) Strategy launched in 2006. Dubbed the *"Green Program"*, the initiative was triggered by the 11th five-year plan of China's Ministry of Environmental Protection, which aimed to reduce the energy consumption per GDP unit by 20% and the emission of major pollutants by 10% across all businesses in China within 5 years. The SASAC's response to the plan was to set the objective of reducing carbon emissions by 40% for all of the organizations under its umbrella. The result was the launch of the *Green Action Plan* in 2007 that advocated the adoption of an extensive array of information technologies (e.g., IP technology for networking, intelligent energy consumption monitoring systems, low-carbon alternatives for IT hardware, e-billing and electronic point of sales systems, etc.) for the purpose of energy conservation, reducing carbon emissions, increasing materials efficiency, and reducing waste.

Nearly four years on, China Mobile's *Green Action Plan* is proving to be an unmitigated success beyond all initial expectations. By 2009, China Mobile had already achieved a 14% reduction in energy consumption and a 49% reduction in carbon emissions across all of its business units, well exceeding the targets set by the SASAC nearly a year before its deadline. Today, China Mobile is an important member of the United Nations Global Compact's Caring for Climate Program and the first and only mainland Chinese corporation to be recognized on the Dow Jones Sustainability Index. But what is most significant about China Mobile's achievements is that it has not only met its environmental objectives, but achieved significant cost savings; by enhancing its logistics, materials management, and work processes (e.g., Yang *et al.*, 2009), and reputational benefits as well (e.g., the organization was also awarded the title of *"China's Top Ten Businesses in Energy Conservation"* from the China Energy Conservation Association in 2010), achieving what has been termed as the triple bottom line (Porter and Kramer 2006, p. 82).

Much of its success has been attributed to the way China Mobile marshaled the collective resources and energies of the major suppliers and customers within its business network towards its environmental aims (China Mobile, 2010a, 2010b). This process of attaining and enacting green leadership in turn, unfolded in three distinct phases.

Establishing a Green Vision (2007–2008)

Like most profit-oriented firms, prior to its efforts at establishing a concerted environmental protection program, China Mobile's emphasis was on economic, as opposed to environmental objectives. Consequently, when the decision was made that environmental objectives had to be formally included in its corporate strategy in response to the objectives set by the Chinese government and the SASAC, the senior management of China Mobile realized that the first thing they had to do is to establish a green vision — an awareness and a vision for environmental protection that is shared throughout the organization.

To this end, China Mobile first established a *Green Action Plan* working team and tasked the team with the responsibility of engaging the key business and provincial units under its corporate umbrella to develop a blueprint for meeting the objectives set by the SASAC. The working team then set about its task by first identifying a number of issues; including establishing organizational environmental standards, implementing energy-saving technologies, pursuing materials efficiency, nurturing a green organizational culture, and creating an environmentally-friendly workplace (China Mobile, 2010b), as well as the internal stakeholders that would be responsible for implementing and managing the change associated with these issues. This was followed by extensive discussions between the working team and the relevant stakeholders as the identified issues were clarified, and detailed action plans were developed and iteratively refined for each business or provincial unit. The overall result of these actions was the development of a detailed organizational environmental strategy that delineated a number of critical environmental priorities, complementing the economic objectives of its original corporate strategy. The existing situation prior to the establishment of the green vision, the activities undertaken to this end, and the implications of those activities are summarized in Table 1.

Enacting Internally, Promoting Externally (2008–2009)

With a detailed organizational environmental strategy in place, China Mobile, with the *Green Action Plan* working team as its executive arm, began pursuing two distinct initiatives. The first initiative was centered on executing the environmental strategy with the internal implementation of

Table 1.   Establishing a Green Vision

Existing Situation	
Emphasis on economic objectives	*"For us in strategic planning, our (previous) emphasis was on investments, income, costs and how to do more with less. Energy conservation was a factor but it was just a secondary concern. In other words, we were more focused on our priorities, but it's 'nice' if we can conserve energy on the side."* — Project Manager, Operations and Network Support

Activities Undertaken	
Formation of the *Green Action Plan* working team	*"In response to the strategic plans of the Government and the SASAC, the organization decided that we would follow suit... The Green Action Plan working team was set up as a crucial link in a 'tower of strength'. Directions come from the top but have to trickle down to the bottom, and the working team would be the conduit that facilitates concrete actions at the operational level."* — Manager (Strategic Planning), Green Action Plan Working Team
Identification of issues and responsible stakeholders	*"We identified issues (and the business units responsible for them) in a number of areas, including primary facilities management (e.g., network infrastructure) and supporting facilities management (e.g., office building). We also identified a number of issues related to our operations ... in areas related to recycling, waste management, and information related to energy conservation."* — Senior Executive, Green Action Plan Working Team
Consultative approach to establish strategic coherence	*"The working team will consult each and every business unit to hammer out a concrete plan of action. They will tell us what they hope to achieve and we will let them know if their suggestions are in line with our department's needs. The first priority is in meeting the fundamental needs of the business units. After that, they might have further suggestions on how we could improve and we would work together to refine those ideas. The key is to ensure that even after implementing these (environmental) objectives, we do not compromise on the needs of our customers and internal stakeholders."* — Data Manager, Home and Corporate Products Center

(Continued)

Table 1. (*Continued*)

Implications of Activities	
Balance between economic and environmental objectives	*"There were many new initiatives as a result of the Green Action Plan ... but we approached them from the angle of cost reduction; we approached them from the angle of increasing efficiency; we incorporated many (monetary) considerations and executed them as a single strategy."* — Manager (Strategic Planning), Green Action Plan Working Team

Green IT initiatives within China Mobile. Prior to the development of the organizational environmental strategy, environmental awareness and responsibility were often manifested in initiatives that were efficiency-oriented (e.g., using fewer resources to reduce wastage). While these initiatives do contribute to environmental protection, the management of China Mobile realized that the organization as a whole has to do more if it was to have the intended deep and far-reaching impact on the environment.

To this end, the *Green Action Plan* working team first sought to induce changes in the culture, corporate values and norms of the organization with extensive awareness and promotional campaigns so as to create an environment that was conducive to the implementation of green IT initiatives. Following this, the working team then established Key Performance Indicators (KPIs) for the key areas identified in organizational environmental strategy. The challenges for the working team in this task were to manage the dialectic tension between effect and attainability, as well as to assign responsibility for meeting the relevant KPIs to the most appropriate internal stakeholder. The KPIs were then presented to the relevant stakeholders and iteratively refined with their inputs. The set of KPIs was an important instrument in formalizing an agreement and gaining the buy-in of the senior managers of the various business units. Overall, these actions helped to re-orientate the business units toward more strategic and effectiveness-oriented environmental initiatives to complement their initial emphasis on efficiency. Some of the effectiveness-oriented green IT initiatives implemented in this phase include the use of IP technology in their telecommunication networks, the installation of IT-based intelligent ventilation, cooling, and power control systems, as well as the use of environmentally-friendly materials in the construction and packaging of their hardware, network, and communication devices. Table 2 provides a summary of the existing situation prior to the internal implementation of Green IT initiatives, the activities undertaken to facilitate this initiative and the implications of those activities.

As in the case of the first, the second initiative was driven by the realization that it will be difficult to attain the intended impact on the environment with China Mobile acting on its own. The management of China Mobile believed that the collective resources of the entities in its business network (including suppliers, customers, and business partners) could be

Table 2.   Enacting Internally

Existing Situations

Emphasis on efficiency as opposed to effectiveness	*"Our (previous) concept of Green (IT) was centered on efficiency... To us, Green IT would be something like a video conferencing system. Before, when we have a meeting in Beijing, we would fly one or two representatives from our 31 provincial offices over. So with video conferencing, we would increase our efficiency greatly... in terms of reducing the amount of resources we used."*

— Project Manager, Operations and Network Support

Activities Undertaken

Inducing changes in culture, values and norms	*"To induce a cultural change, a mindset change within the organization... we launched programs like the 'Green Movement 199.' 199 means 'long-term' (in mandarin)... it was an internal campaign to promote awareness. We can't force people to turn off the lights, print in duplex, turn off all power sources and so on... but we can encourage and educate them... We also organized internal competitions for energy conservation, and competitions for the best energy saving ideas... We printed brochures and posters... set up booths with panel presentations... We sent reminder emails and text messages... We want to embed environmental consciousness in the daily lives of our employees."*

— Manager (Strategic Planning), Green Action Plan Working Team

(*Continued*)

Table 2. *(Continued)*

Establishing appropriate KPIs	*"We (the working team) created a comprehensive set of environmental KPIs based on the action plan and disseminated the KPIs that are relevant to the appropriate business units. The first thing a department manager will have to do is to verify if the KPIs are reasonable, and if they are relevant to his department because many of the KPIs are composite measures that could involve multiple business functions... It was an iterative process of negotiation and refinement..."* — Manager (Green Action Plan), Beijing Branch Office
Gaining the commitment of senior business unit managers	*"After we have our KPI meeting with the Green Action Plan Working Team from headquarters, we will hold a 'Green Action Plan Planning and Initiation Meeting' to develop a plan for meeting those objectives. The top managers and all the vice-presidents of our office are all involved in the planning process. The implementation of our Green (IT) initiatives is initiated in this manner: in the most formal possible way."* — Manager (Green Action Plan), Beijing Branch Office

Implications of Activities

Achieving balance between efficiency and effectiveness	*"In our new direction... we are looking for long-term (as opposed to short-term) cost reductions. Our priority is achieving 'minimal cost, maximum effect.' We hope that with the use of Green (IT), we can reduce energy waste... but we take a more strategic view... We (now) feel that the Green Action Plan can (not only create efficiencies in isolated business processes, but) reduce the operating costs of the entire organization as a whole."* — Senior Executive, Green Action Plan Working Team

leveraged for economies of scale and synergistic outcomes. Consequently, the second initiative was centered on promoting its environmental ideals to these network partners so as to prime them for subsequent mobilization towards its environmental cause.

As most of its network partners were less environmentally conscious, like China Mobile before it embarked on its green program, their priorities were on profitability and their own self-interests. As such, China

Mobile realized that to get its network partners to adopt its environmental ideals as their own, it would first have to induce a mindset change. To do this, China Mobile first attempted to align the goals of its network partners with its own. This was carried out by getting internal stakeholders who were interacting with the network partners to present the economic and environmental benefits of its green IT initiatives, and help them to establish green IT objectives of their own. Following this, China Mobile sought to establish formal incentive and enforcement mechanisms to ensure that its network partners would work towards meeting those objectives. These mechanisms included environmental competitions, recognition for green IT exemplars, an energy conservation rating scale, and improvement targets tied to contractual renewals. With these mechanisms established, China Mobile would then secure the commitment of its network partners by establishing formal collaborative arrangements in the form of contracts or memorandums of understanding. The overall consequence of these actions was that China Mobile was able to influence many of its key network partners to incorporate collective environmental objectives into their corporate strategies. The existing situation prior to the promotion of its environmental ideals, the activities undertaken for this purpose, and the implications of those activities are summarized in Table 3.

Acting in Concert (2009–Present)

The internal enactment of green IT initiatives provided China Mobile with invaluable implementation experience, demonstrable results, and the legitimacy to lead its network partners by example. The external promotion of its environmental ideals, on the other hand, created awareness, provided an indication of China Mobile's commitment to environmental protection, and primed its network partners for collaboration. With these facilitating factors clicking in place, China Mobile was now in the position to lead its network in the implementation of collective green IT initiatives.

Before the implementation of its green program, collective initiatives between China Mobile and its network partners were typically

Table 3. Promoting Externally

Existing Situation	
Emphasis of network entities was on self-interest	*"(Previously,) if we wanted our business partners' cooperation in solving 'Green' issues, we had to provide them with the solution... The solution would have to be attractive to them and aligned with their interests before they would accept the idea. So when we propose the solution, we would have to provide them with a lot of quantitative statistics to demonstrate this (alignment with partners' interests)."* — Senior Executive, Green Action Plan Working Team
Activities Undertaken	
Aligning the goals of network partners with their own	*"We tell our business partners our environmental goals and help them establish their own in alignment with ours... Over time, they have come to realize that these goals benefit them as well. They can tell their other customers that they have achieved China Mobile's environmental standards ... this enhances them credibility."* — Manager (Green Action Plan), Beijing Branch Office
Establish incentive and enforcement mechanisms	*"We would establish competitions to motivate our stakeholders. We have a 'Most Advanced Energy Conservator' award for 4 categories of stakeholders and the prize money is about RMB ¥80,000... Partners who have achieved our highest environmental standards will be cited as model cases for others to emulate."* — Manager (Green Action Plan), Beijing Branch Office *"We have formal contracts with environmental objectives that are renewable in 2 years and we will set them (network partners) targets for improvement. For example we would want them to improve by 10% or 20% (in terms of energy reduction)."* — Manager (Strategic Planning), Green Action Plan Working Team
Formalization of collaborative arrangement	*"In 2009, China Mobile signed 53 suppliers onto a strategic memorandum of understanding, making them official partners of its Green Action Plan"* (China Mobile, 2010b, p. 36).
Implications of Activities	
Achieving a balance between self and collective interest among network entities	*"The balance between their (network entities') self-interest and the interest of everyone is key... For example, a supplier might implement a (Green IT) initiative... If cost savings result, the cost savings will be split between the two parties. It benefits them because this increases their income ... but it contributes towards the collective goal of environmental protection as well."* — Manager (Green Action Plan), Beijing Branch Office

premised on control, governance, and the principle of *'give-and-take'*. However, the management of China Mobile was not satisfied with this *'control-and-react'* mode of collaboration as they believed it created a tendency for satisficing and minimal commitment among its network partners. Consequently, in the implementation of collective green IT initiatives, China Mobile sought to foster a symbiotic and mutually reinforcing mode of collaboration based on equity and proactivity instead. To this end, China Mobile's first order of business was to create a sense of joint-ownership over the collective green IT initiatives by emphasizing to its network partners that their brand and reputation were at stake as well. In addition, China Mobile also provided their network partners with resources, infrastructure, and training to develop their capabilities, which in turn enhanced their abilities to participate and contribute to the collective cause. Following this, China Mobile would also encourage its partners to exercise their enhanced capabilities by engaging them in joint innovations in the production of collective green IT initiatives. Overall, these actions promoted self-organization and voluntarism that enabled China Mobile to adopt a coordinating role and intervene only when necessary. More importantly, these factors enabled the implementation of collective green IT initiatives on a variety of fronts, allowing China Mobile to take a significant step towards achieving the deep and far-reaching environmental impact that it had hoped to achieve. Some of the collective green IT initiatives undertaken in this phase include a network infrastructure joint construction project, a city-level building energy consumption monitoring project, the establishment of industry energy conservation standards, and the organization of a *Green Action Plan* industrial cooperation forum (China Mobile, 2011). Table 4 provides a summary of the existing situation prior to the implementation of collective green IT initiatives, the activities undertaken to facilitate this purpose, and the implications of those activities.

Table 4. Acting in Concert

Existing Situation	
Collective action was directed and 'transaction-like'	*"Before we had the Green Action Plan, our collaboration (with network partners) were transaction-like. If they wanted to collaborate with us ... they would say 'our products superior', 'our prices are lower', 'our quality is higher'... These are tangible parameters that formed the rules of engagement. We would then incentivize them and control them based on these tangible measures."*
	— Manager (Strategic Planning), Green Action Plan Working Team
Activities Undertaken	
Creating a sense of ownership for partners over collective activities	*"We try to make our partners realize that this concerns their brand and reputation as well. This is an incentive for them to take ownership. We would drive some Green (IT) projects, but sometimes, they would push us to work with them as well. So we don't have to resort to hard measures to coerce them to cooperate ... they would take the initiative as well."*
	— Senior Executive, Green Action Plan Working Team
Facilitating the development of partner's capabilities	*"China Mobile helped us to develop the capabilities required for our own Green (IT) initiatives... For example, in an energy consumption monitoring project, we used meters that transmitted data wirelessly with GPRS but this was unreliable. China Mobile provided us with a GRE* (Generic Routing Encapsulation) *Tunnel as an alternative. This made data transmission reliable... This made the project work..."*
	— Chief Engineer, China Construction Software Research Center (China Mobile's Business Partner)
Joint innovation in the production of collective green IT initiatives	*"... in alliance with Huawei, Ericsson, Motorola, Nokia Siemen Networks, Alcatel-Lucent and 6 other leading equipment suppliers ... China Mobile is (jointly engaging in the) research and development of (a mobile device) packaging solution..."*
	— (China Mobile, 2010a, p. 23)
	"Many of our Green (IT) initiatives today are joint innovations. We would engage in brainstorming exercises over months before deciding on what we would do... These brainstorming exercises would involve our manufacturers and business partners."
	— Data Manager, Home and Corporate Products Center

(Continued)

Table 4. (*Continued*)

Implications of Activities	
Achieving a balance between directed and voluntary collective action	*"With an understanding of what China Mobile is trying to do, our partners have become more proactive in collaboration. For example, we communicate with our suppliers more often now ... once every fortnight, and through a variety of channels. Some of them genuinely care about our objectives and sometimes, they would initiate things voluntarily. Take, for example, a supplier like Huawei. They came to understand our Green Action Plan and they immediately launched a corresponding Energy Conservation and Emissions Reduction initiative helmed by a working group to work with us."*

— Senior Executive, Green Action Plan Working Team

References

China Mobile. "Green, we are in action." China Mobile Communications Corporation, Beijing, China, 2010a.

China Mobile. "*Growing harmoniously together: 2009 Corporate Social Responsiblity Report.*" China Mobile Communications Corporation, Beijing, China, 2010b.

Corbett, J. "Unearthing the value for green IT," *ICIS 2010 Proceedings*, 2010 (available online at http://aisel.aisnet.org/icis2010_submissions/198).

Elliot, S. "Transdisciplinary perspectives on environmental sustainability: A resource base and framework for IT-enabled business transformation," *MIS Quarterly* (35:1) 2011, pp. 197–236.

Fortune Magazine "China Mobile Communications," *Fortune Global 500 2010: The World's Largest Companies*, 2010 (available online at http://money.cnn. com/magazines/fortune/global500/2010/snapshots/10935.html).

Porter, M.E. and Kramer, M.R. "Strategy & society: The link between competitive advantage and corporate social responsibility," *Harvard Business Review* (84:12) 2006, pp. 78–92.

Yang, T., Hu, Y., Zheng, P., and Pamlin, D. Low carbon telecommunication solutions in China: Current reductions and future potential WWF China, Beijing, China, 2009.

Discussion Questions

1. What does the extant literature say about green IT?
2. What are the challenges or specifically conflicts in strategic focus that an organization may face when implementing green initiatives, both internally and externally?
3. What are the crucial phases that an organization has to go through while implementing green practices within the organization, and what are the activities that China Mobile case study suggests in these phases, for an effective implementation?
4. Collaboration and collective action among diverse stakeholders beyond the boundaries of a single organization can enhance the reach and magnitude of the impact of green IT implementation (Corbett, 2010; Elliott, 2011). What are the steps that an organization with motivation and ability to leverage on its business network, can follow in order to achieve and exercise green leadership?

Beijing Capital International Airport Terminal 3

Jenson Goh and Mei-Yun Zuo

Background

An airport terminal's main revenue streams can be broadly classified into aeronautical (from airlines) and non-aeronautical (from passengers) streams. In recent years, the industry has become highly competitive with every airport terminal company looking into ways to improve its services and its terminal's capacity. The aim is to become the "travel" hub for airlines and passengers in its region. This is also the company's vision of the state-owned Beijing Capital International Airport (BCIA) Company Limited that manages the main airport of Beijing, China. The main airport of Beijing owned by BCIA consists of three terminals namely, Terminal 1, 2, and 3. Terminal 1 was built in 1990 occupying around 90,000 m². Terminal 2 is 3.7 times larger (336,000 m²) than Terminal 1 and was completed in 1999 to take over Terminal 1 while it was closed for refurbishment. Terminal 1 reopened in 2004 at about the same time where the construction of Terminal 3 began. Constructed specially for the 2008

Olympics Games, Terminal 3 occupies a colossal space of 986,000 m². When completed in March 2008, Terminal 3 was the largest airport terminal in the world.

> "Capital airport is China's first gate to the world. During the period of the Olympics, it takes on the responsibility and honor of being the first customer contact point for athletes and VIPs from all over the world ... the impression that the airport leaves on the visitors represents the hospitality and congeniality of the country..." Mr. Hu Jintao, Chinese President (Translated from the book *The 52nd Gold Medal*)

To achieve the goal of seamless customer touch points across all facets of airport operation in Terminal 3 laid down by President Hu, IT became the imperative enabling tool.

The IT department of BCIA has been the key driving force behind the planning and management of all IT projects, day-to-day terminal operations, and IT personnel (in-house and outsourced staff) in the existing Terminals 1 and 2. Hence, it is not surprising that the department is given the important responsibility to manage the entire Terminal 3 IT projects implementation. In this case study, we present four representative systems implementation in the Terminal 3 program (as shown in Table 1). These systems are selected for this case study because it is among one of the most complex systems undertaken by the BCIA IT department. It is most complex because of its large scale and of its involvement of a large number of internal and external stakeholders. For the system to be successful, the system must not only be delivered on time but also be adopted by all stakeholders readily.

Airport Operation Database (AODB)

Right in the beginning of 1999 when the first AODB (developed by Motorola) was put into use in Terminal 2, the IT department already faced significant challenge in learning the right way to maintain and use it. Over the years, they continued to acquire valuable knowledge about AODB through the constant interaction with vendors like Motorola and through usage and experimentation during operation. As a result, the IT

Table 1.   Brief Background of IT System Implementations

System Name	Brief System Background
Airport Operation Database (AODB)	The "core hub" that allows information captured within other systems in the airport to be seamlessly stored, analyzed, and shared to ensure the smooth running of all aspects of its operations (a.k.a the "heart" of the airport operations).
Airport Departure	System that manages the entire process of checking in and boarding of the passengers and their luggage which all airlines in Terminal 3 are required to use.
Airport Security	System that handles all forms of security-related processing within Terminal 3. Security system of the airport can be classified into 5 levels of security checks (Airport-int, 2009). Due to the huge number of country leaders and foreign visitors involved during the Olympic Games in 2008, the highest level, security 5, was mandated in Terminal 3.
Airport Data Centre	System that facilitates the billing for services rendered in Terminal 3 by the BCIA. From BCIA's perspective, this system demands one of the highest priorities because it deals with the company's revenue-generating activity.

department developed its own set of standard operating procedures that laid the foundation for the future administration and maintenance of AODB in all its airport terminals.

"From 2000 to 2002, we came up with a maintenance standard operation procedure handbook. Till today, our maintenance strategy is dependent on this handbook."

— Deputy Manager, IT Department

In 2004, frequent hardware failures occurred that brought down the AODB in Terminals 1 and 2. The downtime highlighted the dependency of terminal operations and AODB and the need to closely monitor both. Two command centers, namely Terminal Operational Command Centre (TOCC) and System Operational Command Centre (SOCC), were established in late 2007 and all the existing AODB system and terminal operations especially in Terminal 3 were being subsumed under these two command centers. The implementation of a new AODB system in Terminal 3 started in 2006 and was delivered in early 2008. Several key challenges were presented: (1) the new AODB was an off-the-shelf system that differed significantly from the customized AODB built for Terminals 1 and 2; and (2) the information systems in the Airport Transport Control (ATC) which AODB draws its information from were also undergoing upgrade, which led to many uncertainties on how the two systems should interface. The heavy investment in IT staff training by the IT department paid off. Some of the key initiatives that are still in place are: (1) the encouragement of the leaders of the IT staff to build up their knowledge on AODB since 1999; and (2) the cultivation of a strong learning and sharing environment that facilitates the exchange of knowledge across generations of AODB administrator (currently at its fourth generation).

"... our IT department had a very strong learning culture... In 2000, I took the lead with a few other colleagues to look into system backup and business continuity in-depth study (for the AODB) ... during that time, we didn't leverage upon outside help and we did all the research on our own ... we invented many system maintenance strategies."

— Deputy Manager, IT Department

This strong learning and sharing environment encourages desirable behaviors such as selfless sharing of valuable knowledge and proactive problem-solving with "no-blame" culture. The selfless sharing of knowledge is exemplified through the informal mentor–apprentice relationships in the IT department, whereby the past AODB administrator serves as mentor to the new AODB administrator.

"We have an unofficial master-apprenticeship mechanism and a backup mechanism ... if the apprentice is good at work, the master will have opportunity to do other things and can also be promoted. This serves as a big motivation for the master (to coach the apprentice)."

— Chief Engineer (1st Generation AODB Administrator), IT Department

Leaders of the IT department place great trust into the hands of the highly experienced AODB administrators to drive the Terminal 3 project.

In comparison, while the vendor was not expected to perform as well as the IT department staff, they were highly trusted in their ability to deliver quality IT solutions largely due to the close working relationships that had been established during the AODB implementations for Terminals 1 and 2.

"Because of our in-depth knowledge of T2's (Terminal 2) business operation, we can easily make a comparison between T2 and T3 (Terminal 3) and highlight the weakness and strength of T2's system (AODB system), then we can use this knowledge to inform the vendors to improve their system by absorbing T2's strength and eliminating its weakness. In this way, our T3 design (of AODB) can be more aligned with our most ideal maintenance process which was not possible in the past (in T2 AODB)."

— Business Process Lead, AODB System Project

Airport Departure System

The development work of the airport departure system of Terminal 3 started in 2006 and was completed in early 2008. To achieve widespread IT adoption by partners of BCIA (i.e., all the airlines), the IT department adopted a number of key strategies: (1) Inclusion of the highly experienced staff of all the airlines to ensure accurate depiction of each airline's requirement in the tender specification; (2) Assignment of several senior experts (all having over 10 years of experience, including those who were involved in the development of Terminals 1 and 2's departure systems) from the IT department to the project; and (3) Collaboration with a vendor that had more than 50 years of airport departure system implementation experience. As a result, the IT department was able to reap a number of key benefits: (1) Ability to draft out very accurate and detailed business requirements needed for the system implementation, which in turns kept any subsequent changes at bay; (2) Alignment of shared goals to serve passengers between the airlines and IT staff, which encouraged selfless contribution to this common end; and (3) Development of strong trusting relationships among IT and airlines staff. However, the same level of trust appeared to be lacking between the IT department and the vendor, largely because customized development work was done overseas, the software used was proprietary, and only local members, who were less experienced, of the vendor were available onsite for installation and configuration.

"If you have a chance to read the requirement submitted (for the departure system) by each airline, you will be surprised to realize how deep into the future they have predicted for the airline industry to go into development and the needs of their passengers... Because our customers are airlines, the requirement gathered from them are all very accurate in predicting the eventual use."

— Technical Lead, Departure System Project

"They (vendor) guard their technical knowledge strictly ... and because their technology is proprietary and not open-sourced ... we honestly feel that this is not a healthy development into our future relationship."

— Technical Lead, Departure System Project

A series of training sessions was conducted by the IT department to impart important information pertaining to BCIA's culture, practices, work attitudes, and standards to the vendor before implementation commenced. This was to ensure that the vendor got a clear interpretation of the tender's expectation and was able to assimilate seamlessly into the BCIA's culture and working norms.

"We provide training to their (vendor) project management team to impart knowledge about our company's management philosophy, procedure and specific thing to take note of when it comes to system requirement. The objective is to ensure that they can reach up to the same standard as our internal IT staff and to align their way of thinking with ours."

— Technical Lead, Departure System Project

To mitigate the risk of the low trust level of the vendor, the "Backward Planning" (interpreted as setting hard deadline for project and planning backward to set milestones) methodology was adopted to communicate expected deliverables and their deadlines. A weekly meeting was held to track the development progress with major stakeholders and vendors. On a daily basis, a more rigorous schedule of workload was drafted and the local members of the vendor were expected to follow and complete them accordingly. Some members of the IT department staff were stationed beside the vendors to ensure conformance of the daily schedule and to ensure the quality of the task completed.

Airport Security System

The tender for the implementation of this system was awarded in October 2005 and the system went live on March 2008. The requirement to achieve maximum security at level 5 posed significant risk to the system implementation process mainly because the scale of the implementation was unprecedented then in the world in 2008. Many unknowns existed and a large number of stakeholders were involved in this project (such as custom department, airlines, ground staff, etc.). To mitigate this risk, a significant amount of time was spent before October 2005 visiting many vendors around the world to acquire their knowledge in the implementation of the security system.

> "As far as security is concerned, this system is first of its kind in China… In April 2005 before the beginning of the tender, we did a number of visit and research on a number of airports … we involved the design unit in T2 (Terminal 2) to consolidate our findings into the tender specification for the security system in T3 (Terminal 3)."
>
> — Project Manager, Security System Project

While the system implementation posed huge potential risk, it did not faze the members of the staff involved because: (1) they were happy to be associated with the "novel" of the level 5 security system in the world; and (2) they relish in their national pride of having been proven to achieve something seemingly impossible, at all cost no less, through the collective determination of multiple stakeholders.

> "The success of this project relies on our common working attitude. This doesn't just apply to us (IT Department) but the vendor as well. One of our vendor member's wife was giving birth during that time, he chose to stay onsite."
>
> — Project Manager, Security System Project

The overall lack of experience in implementing a system at this level of security raises questions about the skill set of everyone involved. This resulted in a low-trust environment where tight control measures have to be put in place. To ensure proper conformance of the system requirement, a separate audit team was formed to inspect all the project deliverables. The implementation of the system can proceed only after the approval of the audit team. In addition, the IT department also mandated the staff involved to stay onsite during the entire system development period. Frequent site inspection and weekly meetings were conducted to instill the sense of urgency and to get things done right the first time. To ensure no opportunism behavior of the vendors and staff, a joint responsibility deposit was imposed on them, which mandated the timely completion of task or the risk of losing portion or all of the deposit. In addition, payments to the vendors were done in a "milestone" fashion, i.e., they got paid only when the audit team certified that they have met all the requirements of that milestone.

> "Our company adopts an outcome driven control, that is to say if you achieve your target, you will be given monetary reward, if you don't, money is deducted ... once we established the target, everyone will come up with the "responsibility" deposit, you don't hit it (target) we deduct money from the deposit. You complete it, we give you reward."
>
> — Project Manager, Security System Project

The leaders in the IT department have led by example. They held progress meeting on Saturday and conducted inspection at night to instill the discipline of working round the clock. In addition, the Chinese believed in encouragement slogan. Many were placed around the premises to motivate all the stakeholders to answer to the higher calling of their work. For example, one of the slogans in Chinese posted at the canteen, translated to the following effect: "*If you are afraid of death, don't become a communist. If you are afraid of hard work, don't take up system development work of T3!*"

Data Center System

The implementation of the data centre system started in late 2007 and was delivered within six months in March 2008. As the main purpose of this system was to provide a single authoritative source of bill calculation for all the internal stakeholders of BCIA, it must be precise and error-free. This was not easily achievable. The IT department was aware of the difficulty involved in getting buy-ins from internal stakeholders, so one of its most well-respected IT staff within the airport was assigned as the project manager. Through close coordination and many intense negotiations with all the stakeholders, the BCIA project manager was able to keep the implementation effort moving. To further accelerate the development of the system, the BCIA project manager leveraged upon his close working relationship with the local partners at the Company CX (A large multinational company) to start work on the project before the signing of the tender document was finalized. To ensure a tight control on changes, a rigorous change management process was implemented. Despite all these preventative measures imposed to get the project completed on time, the project manager still faced a number of difficult challenges including: (1) Coping with the withdrawal of CX from the tender before the actual signing of the tender document. This was a crisis especially since the local vendor of CX had already committed their resources into this project. The quick thinking project manager managed to resolve the situation by convincing the local vendor to absorb the staff deployed onsite by CX, so as to minimize disruption; (2) Coping with three unforeseen change requests during the development of the system. If they were mandated to complete before the Olympics, these changes would cause the system schedule to overrun. The project manager mitigated the situation by convincing the stakeholders to defer the changes after the 2008 Olympics after some intense negotiations; and (3) Coping with the request to subsume the two functionalities embedded within the Terminal Operation Database system and the Company's ERP System into the new system. This would disrupt the established information flow and power structure within an organization derived from these two systems. Leveraging upon his respectable status and given complete authority by the management, the project manager managed to navigate an extremely delicate change process which enabled the smooth transition of the multiple stakeholders from their familiar interfaces to this new system.

"During the system development process, we have been given a lot of authority to control many decisions concerning payment and operational data which include daily operation report … from our angle, this makes a lot of our work easier to implement."

— Project Manager, Data Centre System Project

The project manager was able to overcome these challenges because of the following measures: (1) Constant and persistent communication about the accounting regulatory requirements that BCIA needs to conform to and the key advantages and improvements which the new system could provide; (2) Weekly meeting to trace the progress and report it back to the stakeholders; and (3) Verified payment to the vendor only when a milestone was completed and signed off by him. Furthermore, due to the project manager's willingness to engage the local vendor despite the withdrawal of the main potential contractor (CX), the vendor's project manager was willing to give something in return to the project manager's trust. For example, he was very proactive in reporting the status of the project and was flexible to take up *ad hoc* work of a smaller scale not specified within the initial terms of contract. He did these jobs at no extra cost to BCIA.

"… The core team (vendor team) comprises of team members that possess in-depth business domain knowledge and strong technical skills and experiences in this area (development of Data Centre) … you don't need to explain things in detail to them (vendor) … if we have another vendor, the pressure on us would be really great and we will probably have to do OT everyday".

— Project Manager, Data Centre System Project

Comparatively, the internal partners (such as airlines and shop owners) were much less "cooperative" with the IT department's project manager than the vendor. Consequently, the trust level of these partners is low.

"If you don't have professionals to control the process of this project, the project risk would be high. If you let the users (partners) control the process, you will face the challenge of frequently changing requirements … because they (partners) represent their own interest."

— Project Manager, Data Centre System Project

The 52nd Gold Medal in Olympics

As 2008 Olympics games came to an end, the athletes and VIPs head home via the massive and impressive Beijing Capital International Airport (BCIA) Terminal 3. The years of hard work of the BCIA IT department paid off. The myriads of IT systems (small and large scale) were not only rapidly adopted by all the stakeholders when they were rolled out in 2008, everyone worked closely to ensure the operational works in Terminal 3 were seamless throughout the time of the Olympic games.

To commemorate the IT department's capabilities in accomplishing a seemingly impossible mission, a book titled "The 52nd Gold Medal" was published and distributed to all staff in BCIA. In the eyes of the Chinese government, they felt the BCIA IT department's achievements are equivalent to winning the 52nd gold medal in the Olympics Games for China. This is the greatest honor that can be given to any one organization by the Chinese government.

Looking back at this case, one cannot help but wonder how the BCIA IT department (with a manpower strength of around 150) is able to pull off this Terminal 3 program implementation? Especially given that they can only spare half of their manpower (around 70) for this program implementation while the remaining staff worked to ensure existing operations in Terminals 1 and 2 run smoothly. What are the reasons behind their success in getting all the IT systems in Terminal 3 readily adopted by all stakeholders in such a short period of time?

Discussion Questions

1. Identify all the risks in each of the IT system in the Terminal 3 program and the consequences of these failures.
2. What is agile IT adoption practice? What is the role of agile IT adoption practices in helping BCIA completing the Terminal 3 program implementation on time and on schedule? What constitutes a practice?
3. For each of the IT system implementation, identify the organization control mechanisms that are being used to mitigate the identified risk. Discuss the trust relationship between the management, staff, and vendors.

Neusoft & SAP China

Derek Wenyu Du

Neusoft

The company is a leading IT service provider in China, with 15,000 staff and 9,000 clients. Less than 2 decades ago, the company was merely a startup incubated at Northeast University with fewer than 10 people — two university professors and their graduate students. Informed by literature review on boundary-spanning, two pertinent attributes should be emphasized: (1) the boundary-spanning capacity, which is manifested in the collective technical and communication skills of Neusoft's workforce; (2) the boundary-spanning strategy, which is manifested in Neusoft's communication structure with clients. Two themes then emerged from the data: One is the relationship between the two attributes, which depicts the alignment outlook; the other is the coevolution between the two attributes, which depicts the alignment process. Accordingly, we organized our data in these two themes.

In terms of the relationship, the company has a technical-extreme workforce and a window-communication structure. The workforce is a result of its technically focused recruitment and training. New members are hired largely for technical merits, and technical training programs are far richer than communication programs. As a senior vice president who oversees the entire Dalian operation noted, the recruitment emphasizes technical skills but not communication skills:

"When we recruit, we don't expect everyone can speak Japanese. For Neusoft, our primary focus is on technology. We need to make sure the people we hire can program well. Intensive coding experience is highly appreciated."

Also, training emphasizes technical upgrade but not communication upgrade. Another senior president who was administering the Toshiba printer OS development project noted as follows:

"We have training courses all year long for our staff to upgrade their skills. They can learn from the very basic programming, such as C, C++, and Java, to the more advanced level, such as enterprise architecture. We also have some communication training, but it is meant for managers who need to meet clients regularly. For the rest, that is not important."

To further strengthen the technical focus, Neusoft established its own IT institute in 2000, the curriculum of which was purely focused on coding. This technically focused recruitment and training can be seen as inheritances of its earlier establishment as a research lab. In fact, the research-lab culture is still deeply cherished by Neusoft's top management (i.e., many are professors). For example, when the company designed its new headquarters in 2000, it chose the campus-style of the low-rise buildings in the suburbs instead of that of the high-profile office towers in the city center, which many domestic ITO vendors were doing in China as a means of boosting the corporate image. When we first arrived at the site, we indeed mistook the office buildings for a university campus. Later, we were told that it was purposely designed to preserve the culture.

The window-communication structure is named after a key role, Window Project Manager (PM), whose primary task is to collect and disseminate information between clients and Neusoft. In most cases, Windows are located at the clients' premise so that they can understand clients' needs better. As a frontier staff, Window PMs must be equipped with good communication skills. An interesting scene was that, whenever a Window PM was present at the interview, the engineers tended to speak less and let the Window dominate the conversation. Good technical know-how, on the other hand, is also needed, because Windows are also required to communicate with internal engineers. To this end, Window PMs are in general groomed from technical leaders. An assistant director assisting the senior director to implement strategic decisions explained about how communication is handled by Window PMs:

> "Window PMs are the superstars of the team. They have rich experience in technology and are also aware of Japanese cultures. They have no problem in communication. Sometimes, we hire local Japanese as Window PMs. But those people must also have rich technical background (as well). To assume this role, the individual must be good at both technology and communication."

Another important feature of the window design is that all communication must and can only go through the Window. Engineers are not allowed to communicate with clients directly, and clients, on the other hand, have very limited knowledge about the internal, since the only person they deal with is the Window PM. A permanent party secretary who governing the Toshiba Printer OS Project said about communication be centrally controlled by Window PMs:

> "Not everyone in the team is allowed to communicate with the client. Only Window PM can do so. Information circulation, either outbound or inbound, must go through the Window, who will vet the content and make sure it is professional and the presentation is up to Japanese standards. On the other hand, we don't want clients to see much of the inside. Their contact point should be limited at the Window PM."

In terms of coevolution, Neusoft's workforce and communication structure are aligned through three phases. In Phase 1, the company's main concern was to ramp up its technical capacity. In 1991, most ITO projects were embedded system development, which was coding intensive in nature. Existing lab engineers were often unable to cope with the heavy workload and experienced software engineers were also limited in the market at that time. A major breakthrough of this capacity bottleneck happened when three university-affiliated research labs were lobbied to join the company. Powered by experienced researchers, Neusoft soon established an outstanding engineering team, which was deemed the best in the Northeast region. As a senior Vice President, also one of the founders noted:

> "At the beginning, we needed a lot of experienced and strong technical people. At that time, we were not interested in fresh graduates; we didn't have time or resources to train them. Most engineers then were recruited from the university-affiliated research labs. They are very experienced and competent."

However, in terms of communication structure, it was not clear at that time. Communication could happen through various channels, including translators, project managers, and mostly engineers.

In Phase 2, a clear communication structure was established. In 1996, Neusoft started to move its business from predominately technology solution to include end-to-end business solutions. The ITO partnership with Toshiba was an endeavor in this direction. Requested by Toshiba, Neusoft started to reconfigure its development process, which, at that time, largely followed a loose research-lab style and not suitable for developing business solution. A more standard and professional style was needed. That was when Neusoft started to pick up CMM (i.e., Capability Maturity Model). As part of the reconfiguration, the window-communication structure was decided by the management team, after serious consideration of the strengths and weaknesses of the existing workforce. The new structure was warmly welcomed by not only Toshiba but existing clients, who acknowledged the enhanced communication quality delivered by Window PM. A permanent party secretary who governing the Toshiba Printer OS Project and joining Neusoft in 1994 described:

> "When I joined, there was no standard communication protocol. Communication was rather unregulated. Since 1996, the company had gone through a major transformation. Project management moved from the research-lab style to a more professional style. Window-communication structure was developed at that time. It was largely based on our own strengths and weaknesses."

In Phase 3, the window-communication structure in turn reinforced the technical focus of workforce. In 2000, Neusoft achieved CMM Level 4 and as part of the endeavor, the new window-communication structure was institutionalized across all project teams. Since the structure saved most engineers from communication, communication expectation on engineers was further reduced and technical expectation was raised again. This change, coupled with rapid expansion, demanded an "army of technical-excellent engineers." Although engineering graduates from public schools were many, they often disappointed Neusoft due to the lack of technical focus and aspiration. To fill the gap, the company established its own IT institute in 2000. The curriculum was focused on coding and little on the rest. As a senior director who administered the Toshiba Printer OS Project noted:

"Our outsourcing model (i.e., the Window Communication) requires a lot of good engineers with intensive coding experience. Graduates from the market do not suit our model well as they are trained on a very broad scale. Thus, we built up our own IT institute. The curriculum is purely focused on coding. Students get very solid in writing codes, it is like their second nature, and they can fit in our model very easily."

These graduates, as commented by a top manager, are 'tailor-made' to support window communication.

SAP China

SAP is an internationally renowned IT service provider, with 47,000 employees and clients in over 120 countries. It has multiple subsidiaries across the world, each with their own dynamics. This study focuses on the China subsidiary, which was set up in 1997 to support clients in Asia Pacific and Japan, with the primary focus on Japan. As with the Neusoft case, two themes emerge from the data. In terms of the relationship between workforce and communication structure, SAP reflects an alignment concept very different from that of Neusoft. Its recruitment emphasizes equally both technical and communication skills. Therefore, candidates strong in technology but weak in communication will not be considered. A senior director who takes care of the administration of Global Support China Center noted:

"Most of the people we hire tend to, let's say, have double degree, one in a technical area and one in Japanese, or they have worked in Japan for 2, 3 years with a technical degree. The weakest technical hire I would take would be someone who has only majored in Japanese but maybe worked 3 years in Japan in a technical role. That is probably the weakest candidate I will consider. Anything else doesn't work."

Its training also carries a balanced weight on both technology and communication. As a result, the workforce is strong in both technical know-how and communication.

"We focus on and devote a lot of resources to technical training. We occasionally fly in the overseas experts here to deliver technical training. We also send consultants overseas to receive (technical) training. Locally, we assign newcomers a senior consultant as his mentor to constantly groom him/her on the technical aspect."

— Support Manager A, administering message service related to CRM

"The company also has a lot of training on customer interaction. For example, we have a full-time Japanese teacher in-house to deliver language training. She is very familiar with the context we are in, because she used to work for SAP Japan. This relevance is crucial ... the company often invites customer interaction experts from Japan to deliver training and everyone also gets opportunities to rotate to Tokyo office for a while to be immersed into the local culture."

— Support Manager B, administering message service related to Logistic

Nearly every consultant has a strong technical background (e.g., an engineering-related degree), and everyone was able to articulate well. The overall interview experience in SAP China was very different from that in Neusoft. As far as structure is concerned, the company adopts a very open communication. Every individual consultant can communicate with clients directly. For senior consultants, they are also expected to actively approach clients even before issues emerge. Clients, on the other hand, can communicate with different consultants based on the area of issues that they face. For example, a client with a database issue may likely be received by a consultant specialized in database. The senior director, administrating Global Support China Center, explained:

> "We expect everyone to work closely with client and encourage them to jump out of the (internal) boundary and approach clients proactively.... essentially, clients are not served by the same consultant but by multiple consultants... We trust our employees and in general, after 3–6 months training, they are put in front of the client. But of course, they start from basic issues."

Another quality of this open structure is that communication is flexible. For example, an issue can be routed to different individuals if collaboration is needed. In this case, the client may receive an early response from one consultant and a later response from another. Since everyone is proficient in communication, this flexible arrangement runs smoothly. Consultant A who handles CRM-related message said about communication circulated among individuals:

> "The company promotes flexible and collaborative team work. For example, if I feel the issue is better explained through face-to-face, I will route the message to the onsite division. If the onsite consultants need advisory support, they can route the message to advisory division (to call for help). Essentially, all inputs from different divisions are consolidated in the message so that everyone is on the same picture. Eventually, clients may receive the response from any of us, depending on who has the most relevant expertise."

In terms of coevolution between workforce and communication structure, SAP also reflects a very different path to that of Neusoft in Phase 1, the company's main task was to build up the communication structure. In 1997, the management team's major concern was whether this new offshore subsidiary can handle the heavy workload generated by SAP's complicated product line, which ranges from giant ERP used by Fortune 500 to CRM used by Small and Medium Businesses (SMBs).

A message-solving mechanism was designed to facilitate the process: Every time a user needs support, s/he is instructed to submit a message, logging the technical component, priority, and symptoms of the issue; the message is then assigned to a consultant of the relevant technical expertise. This is expected to speed up the process by focusing consultants in a set of technical areas and eliminating middlemen. As Support Manager A who administers message service related to CRM and joined the center at the very beginning recalled:

> "At that time, the primary need was to have a robust delivery model so that we can cope with the overwhelming workload from the Japanese clients... We then established a routing system, whereby issues pertinent to a specific technical area will be routed to the technical expert in that area."

However, despite the good intention, the mechanism failed to produce the expected outcome. At the end of Phase 1, only simple issues from SMB clients were shifted to China and those from enterprise clients still remained in Japan. The reason behind this disappointing outcome was that the China subsidiary did not have enough qualified consultants to fully support the mechanism, which demanded strong technical background and competent communication skill for everyone. This requirement is further raised by Japanese clients, who are scrupulous about details. For example, small bugs are treated as big failures and correspondences with grammatical errors are simply rejected. One of the founders summarized this succinctly, "We are taking the hardest job in IT."

In Phase 2, the situation was changed. In 2004, a new senior director was appointed as the head to speed up the support migration. The very first task on his list was to recruit consultants with both technical and communication skills so that the existing message-solving mechanism can take off. However, the recruitment was very challenging, because in the job market, individuals with both skills were very limited, although individuals with one were many. Three strategies were then adopted. First, the company set up its office in two strategic locations (i.e., Dalian and Shanghai) so that it could access talents in both cities and their regional areas. Second, the company sponsored a double-degree program (i.e., one degree in engineering and the other in Japanese) in Dalian Institute of Technology, the best university in Dalian. The sponsorship allowed SAP to recruit students for internship. Under normal circumstances, interns would stay after their terms. In fact, SAP seldom had problems in wooing the best graduates in China, due to its prestigious brand name. Third, a recruitment campaign was launched in Japan, with the objective of recruiting Japanese-born engineers, who were looking for exciting opportunities in China and Chinese immigrants who had worked in Japan for years and intended to move back. As a senior director who administrates Global Support China Center and joined the center in 2004 noted:

"One can say that we are conducting very high-end recruiting. That is necessary, because, if we relax the standard a little bit, we may get people who actually cannot talk to the Japanese client. In that case, they will probably create all kinds of misunderstandings."

However, even though the new hires were "topnotch", they could not become fully productive until they had gone through an intensive training cycle from 20 months to 3 years. At the end of the year 2008, the center had developed a strong workforce. A few consultants were even recognized as Subject Matter Experts globally in their technical areas. The potential of the message-solving mechanism was thus fully unleashed: over 800,000 issues were solved in that year and client satisfaction was maintained at the same level as when support was delivered by the local Japanese.

In Phase 3, SAP China was ready to do something more ambitious. With the outstanding consultants accumulated in the past years, the management team aspired to enhance client satisfaction to a higher level by upgrading the support paradigm. Under the previous paradigm, support was responsive, since service was not rendered until clients logged a message. Under the new paradigm, support was proactive and some services could be delivered before clients even requested them. This new paradigm was carried out by the establishment of a new division in 2008, called Support Advisory Division (SAD). As a senior manager who administers the SAD described:

"Customer satisfaction is the core value for us. But, it cannot be significantly improved through the existing model. We need a new one that actively drives the client and provides services before they even ask... In 2008, we felt we had accumulated sufficient expertise to do this and my team was thus founded."

SAD proactively assessed client systems and preempted issues. The assessment was often carried out via conference calls, during which clients were invited to share concerns about the system. This initiative required consultants to have excellent communication skills so that they could encourage clients to speak out. Japanese clients were known to be skeptical and quiet when asked to speak. A lot of technical knowledge was also expected so that consultants can quickly identify the issue, and offer prompt response. In general, clients would expect some form of useful feedback right after investing their time in sharing. Therefore, consultants of SAD were mostly Subject Matter Experts, elite of this high-end team. This new initiative was well received by clients. After its launch, a feedback survey showed that client satisfaction reached a new level, exceeding the time when support was provided by the local Japanese. This was a remarkable achievement that few ITO vendors in the Japan–China ITO market could equal.

Discussion Questions

1. What is an effective boundary-spanning? And what is the role of vendors in an effective boundary-spanning in ITO?
2. What are the capacity features of Neusoft? And how can they align their boundary-spanning capacity and strategy?
3. What are the capacity features of SAP China? And how do they align their boundary-spanning capacity and strategy?
4. Can design outlook and design process behind the two vendors' boundary-spanning practice apply to other ITO vendors? And what about non-ITO contexts (e.g., partnership alliances and headquarter–subsidiary relationship)?

Shanghai Tobacco

Barney Tan

Organizational Background

The history of the modern tobacco industry in China can be traced back to over a hundred years when a group of American traders established the first cigarette factory in the city of Tianjin in 1891. Although domestic cigarette production began in the city of Guangzhou just eight years later, foreign tobacco firms maintained their market leadership in the Chinese tobacco industry for over 50 years until the Communist Revolution led to the founding of the People's Republic of China (PRC) in 1949. In the immediate years following the establishment of the PRC, all the existing tobacco firms were brought under government control as the Chinese government sought to unify the tobacco industry under a system of centralized management and monopolistic operations. It was these circumstances that led to the birth of Shanghai Tobacco Company (STC). The initial manifestation of STC was a private tobacco firm named Etsong Tobacco Company that was subjected to a government takeover in 1952. It was renamed Shanghai Cigarette Factory when it became the largest and only cigarette factory of the city of Shanghai in 1960.

87

The government agency established and tasked with the management of the tobacco monopoly system is the State Tobacco Monopoly Administration (STMA), and under its jurisdiction, the China National Tobacco Corporation (CNTC) was established to manage all the tobacco firms, as well as the production, distribution, marketing and sales of all tobacco products in the country in 1982. In line with the political and economic liberalization movement of the early 1980s, the STMA and the CNTC began a four-pronged modernization program centered on the acquisition of new technologies, global expansion, diversification into other industries, and the consolidation of production facilities that effected sweeping changes across the tobacco industry. Under the mandate of the modernization program, Shanghai Cigarette Factory was merged with a state-owned cigarette packaging firm, a state-owned tobacco logistics firm, and the Gaoyang Cigarette Factory to form a vertically integrated, large-scale corporation in 1993. The newly formed entity was renamed STC.

Since its inception, STC has been merged with the Beijing Cigarette Factory and the Tianjin Cigarette Factory to become the largest tobacco corporation under the purview of the CNTC. Today, from raw materials to final delivery, STC has achieved complete vertical integration along the supply chain, managing an extensive network of over 50 tobacco suppliers and 30,000 retailers worldwide. From 22 production facilities across the globe, STC produces a kaleidoscopic array of different cigarettes, ranging from the internationally renowned Chunghwa and Panda cigarettes, to local bestsellers such as Double Happiness, Peony, and South China Sea cigarettes. In 2007, STC's gross profits and net assets were estimated at over US$456 million and US$741 million respectively. In terms of tax contributions, STC is ranked sixth among all corporations in the whole of China.

The achievements of STC are considerable given that it has had to contend with the challenges of a dynamic and unpredictable environment that is precipitated by two primary forces of change. The first stems from the modernization initiatives of the STMA and the CNTC, which intensified following the entry of China into the World Trade Organization (WTO) in 2004 as they sought to cope with the heightened competition caused by the liberalization of international trade. In particular, over the years, the modernization initiatives have led to a dramatic restructuring of the tobacco industry, a host of mergers as smaller and less efficient tobacco firms are merged with the larger and more established firms, a series of new tobacco policies, and a revolutionary national competitive strategy that emphasizes market volume, brand building, and bureaucratic management. The second force of change in the tobacco industry stems from the National Information Program (NIP) (see Loo, 2004; Ma *et al.*, 2005) launched by the Chinese government in the mid-1990s. Aimed at driving industrialization and modernization through the adoption of IT, the NIP provided a strong impetus for government agencies and state-owned enterprises to adopt market-oriented business practices, contemporary management philosophies and cutting-edge IT to enhance their operations. This dynamic environment provided a backdrop of instability and constant change that endured throughout STC's Enterprise Applications (EA) implementation journey.

Phase 1: MRP II Implementation Failure (1993–1994)

Prior to EA implementation, most of the departments and business units at STC were heavily reliant on paper-based information, although a handful of them had developed small systems and applications in isolation, resulting in the formation of "islands of automation" (Peppard, 2007, p. 337) that resided within functional silos with minimal integration. EA implementation at STC began in 1993 with the implementation of BPCS, a Manufacturing Resource Planning (MRPII) package developed by SSA Global. The decision to implement BPCS was made unilaterally by the top management of STC. In contrast, the involvement of the other organizational stakeholders such as the IT personnel within the organization and the business units affected by the implementation, in the decision to implement BPCS was limited. For the IT personnel, it was largely due to their lack of capabilities and authority within the organization as the organizational IT function was not even a formal department within STC at the time. For the business units, it was because of their lack of knowledge on the implications and use of IT.

In fact, the top management similarly did not fully comprehend or appreciate the organizational implications of BPCS implementation. The implementation decision was not driven by strategic insights or operational needs, but was primarily influenced by the coercive, mimetic, and

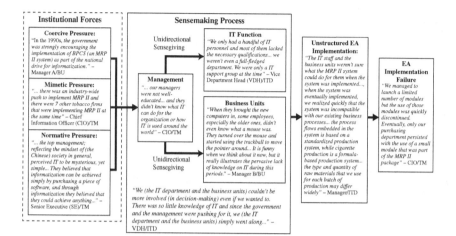

Figure 1. Antecedents, Nature, and Implications of Organizational Sensemaking in Phase 1 (1993–1994).

normative pressures (DiMaggio and Powell, 1983) for EA implementation in the external environment. These institutional forces (Scott, 2001), in turn, stemmed from the "informatization" movement that was rapidly taking hold within the national consciousness at the time. Consequently, the implementation process was unstructured and poorly planned, and when the system went live, STC quickly realized that the system was incompatible with its existing business processes. The misalignment between the structures and processes embedded within BPCS and the existing structures and processes of STC (e.g., Sia and Soh, 2007) was so severe that only a small subset of modules from the software package could eventually be launched, and the use of all but one of the launched modules was quickly discontinued within months. The antecedents, nature, and implications of organizational sensemaking for the nature and outcome of EA implementation at STC during this phase, as well as the corroborating evidence are presented in Figure 1.

Phase 2: "E-Enablement" (1995–1999)

Following the failed implementation of BPCS, the top management of STC felt that it was too difficult to configure a packaged EA to suit its complex, formula-based production system (e.g., the production formula of cigarettes has to be constantly re-adjusted as the quality of each batch of tobacco leaves may differ). Yet, the management did not want to revert to old, paper-based way of working as it would represent a considerable step backwards. Eventually, the decision was made to custom-build an EA that was tailored to its idiosyncratic business processes. The experience of failure also imparted the lesson of the need to include the perspectives of other stakeholders in the process of EA implementation. Consequently, although the top management maintained an active role in directing the overall process of implementation (i.e., by identifying the key business processes for prioritized automation), the newly established IT department was granted considerable autonomy to initiate module development in the areas they deemed important.

The needs of each functional department guided the development of the new custom built EA. Although the implementation process was primarily driven by the top management and the IT department, the business units, equipped with a better understanding of how IT can support its business processes as a result of the experience of the previous phase, worked actively with the IT department to shape the development of the relevant modules when their business processes were identified for automation. However, as the business units had little influence over the overall direction of EA development, and moreover, as the modules were developed in isolation, this arrangement resulted in an effective but unsynchronized form of EA implementation, and the integration between the developed modules was limited. The lack of integration meant that there were little changes to the existing business processes of the organization. The processes were merely automated in a process termed "e-enablement" by the organizational stakeholders. The antecedents, nature, and implications of the sensemaking process for the nature and outcome of EA implementation in the second phase, as well as the supporting evidence are presented in Figure 2.

In Figures 1–4, the source of each quote is labeled in the following format: Designation of Informant/ Stakeholder Group. The three primary stakeholder groups identified as salient to the process of EA implementation at STC are the Top Management (TM), the IT Department (ITD), and the various Business Units (BU).

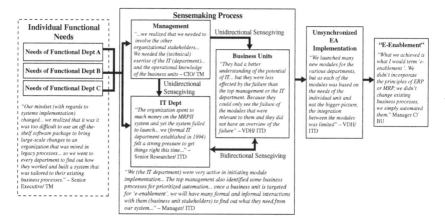

Figure 2. Antecedents, Nature, and Implications of Organizational Sensemaking in Phase 2 (1995–1999).

Phase 3: Systems Integration (2000–2005)

Although STC's business processes were not re-engineered or optimized during the implementation of the custom-built EA, the automation of its business processes nevertheless brought about some measure of efficiency gains. The efficiency gains provided the top management of STC with an indication of the strategic value of the EA, and consequently, they began to view the organizational use of the EA with increasing importance. In particular, the top management envisioned leveraging the EA to improve its business processes and management effectiveness, and streamline STC's organizational structure, and to achieve these objectives, they realized that there was a need for systems integration. Yet, systems integration called for a shift from the unsynchronized approach to EA implementation to an integrated approach that accounted for not just the needs of the individual departments but the overarching needs of the organization as a whole, and the integrated approach was possible only if the various business units involved in a cross-functional business process could shape the supporting module collectively.

Consequently, with the overall needs of the organization guiding the systems integration initiative, the top management and the IT department would first identify the existing system modules for integration, and the cross-functional business processes that were not automated in the previous phase for automation. After the modules and processes were identified, the various business units would actively provide feedback to the top management and the IT department to provide a holistic picture of the organizational needs, and their requirements of the integrated systems throughout the implementation process. As a result of the experience gained from the previous phase, the business unit stakeholders were able to contribute more to the EA implementation process as they had a clearer picture of what they required from the system and how IT can enhance their business processes. In addition, as the IT department was largely credited for the successful implementation of the EA in the previous phase, its standing within the organization was enhanced. The IT department was institutionalized as an IT Information Center and given an expanded advisory role in directing systems development as the top management trusted their technical expertise. This approach to organizational sensemaking led to a coordinated form of EA implementation as the perspectives of a diverse range of organizational stakeholders were reconciled and integrated. The result was the integration of the numerous modules launched in the previous phase into three major systems: A financial system, a sales system, and a resource management system. The antecedents, nature, and implications of organizational sensemaking for EA implementation in Phase 3, as well as the corroborating evidence are presented in Figure 3.

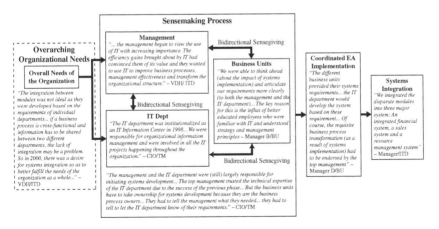

Figure 3. Antecedents, Nature, and Implications of Organizational Sensemaking in Phase 3 (2000–2005).

Phase 4: Strategic EA Integration (2006–Present)

The cumulative experience of the previous phases has led to significant changes among the stakeholder groups involved in EA implementation. By the end of the third phase, the management was significantly more knowledgeable about the organizational implications of EAs (through the experience gained from managing the EA implementation process and leadership renewal), and cognizant of the need to include the perspectives of the IT department and the various business units in initiating and planning for EA development. On the other hand, as a result of their involvement in the process of systems integration, individual business units had learnt to look beyond their own needs and now had a deeper appreciation of the overarching needs and strategic objectives of the organization. In addition, in recognition of the key role it played in the EA implementation success of the previous phases, the IT Information Center was once again accorded with an expanded role in the organization. By 2006, the IT Information Center was known as the Center for Economic Information and was tasked with collecting and analyzing the operational data and statistics of the entire organization.

As a result of these changes, STC was ready to move beyond using its EA to cater to the needs of the organization, to leveraging its EA to support the organization's strategic objectives for the attainment of competitive advantage. With the strategic objectives of the organization guiding systems development, all of the three stakeholder groups were actively involved in shaping and making key decisions about the implementation process. The top management would identify possible areas of development based on their strategic vision and verify the feasibility and utility of their plans with the Center of Economic Information (i.e., the organizational IT function) and the various business units. Likewise, the Center of Economic Information, based on a technical optimization perspective, and the business units, based on their intimate knowledge of the firm's business processes, would identify possible areas for development and verify their plans with one another before submitting their plans to the top management for approval. This approach to organizational sensemaking led to an integrative form of EA implementation as the three stakeholder groups were collectively engaged in shaping the overall implementation process.

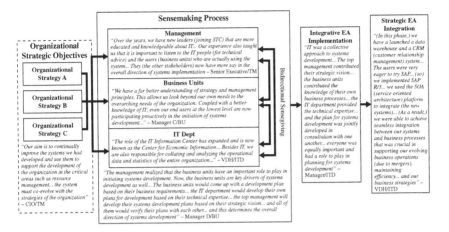

Figure 4. Antecedents, Nature, and Implications of Organizational Sensemaking in Phase 4 (2006–Present).

The integrative approach to EA implementation in turn, resulted in the successive launches of a host of new systems including a data warehouse, a CRM system, and the SAP R/3, that were integrated using a Service-Oriented Architecture (SOA). The various EAs launched were tightly aligned with and in support of the operations and business strategies of STC, and the seamless integration between them provided the organization with greater flexibility as it was able to pick and choose from the functionalities of various EAs that best suited their needs. The antecedents, nature, and implications of organizational sensemaking for the nature and outcome of EA implementation in the fourth phase, as well as the supporting evidence are presented in Figure 4.

References

DiMaggio, P.J., and Powell, W.W. "The iron cage revisited: Institutional isomorphism and collective rationality in organizational fields," *American Sociological Review* (48:2) 1983, pp. 147–160.

Loo, B.P.Y. "Telecommunications reforms in China: Towards an analytical framework," *Telecommunications Policy* (28:9–10) 2004, pp. 697–714.

Ma, L., Chung, J., and Thorson, S. "E-government in China: Bringing economic development through administrative reform," *Government Information Quarterly* (22:1) 2005, pp. 20–37.

Peppard, J. "The conundrum of IT management," *European Journal of Information Systems* (16:4) 2007, pp. 336–345.

Scott, W.R. Institutions and Organizations, (2nd ed.). Sage Publications, Thousand Oaks, CA, 2001.

Sia, S.K. and Soh, C. "An assessment of package-organisation misalignment: Institutional and ontological structures," *European Journal of Information Systems* (16:5) 2007, pp. 568–583.

Weick, K.E. *Sensemaking in Organizations*. Sage, Thousand Oaks, CA, 1995.

Discussion Questions

1. Prior literature has suggested that the nature of organizational sensemaking is a function of the inputs and context of the sensemaking process (Weick, 1995). Based on your understanding of this theorem, what factors do you think lead to the failure of EA implementation in the first phase? (Lecturer can give some hints to the students by briefly discussing what inputs are and what is context of the sensemaking process).

2. Compared with the first phase, what changes had been made in terms of context of sensemaking in the second phase? What benefits do you think would be brought due to those changes? Although e-enablement finally was achieved, there were still some problems embedded in this sensemaking configuration, what is the most severe one?

3. In phase three and phase four, we can find that, all three stakeholders, top management, IT department, and business unit, actively participate in the sensegiving process. Despite this, slight difference still existed between these two phases in the perspective of roles played by the three stakeholders. Illustrate the difference.

4. What conflicts between the EA and organization were encountered by STC in this case during the four phases? How did STC solve those conflicts?

China's E-Government

Adela Chen and Wayne Huang

The central government of China actively promoted the use of IT in the public sector during the late 1990s, which led to municipality governments, such as that in Shanghai, developing their own e-government strategies. Countrywide e-government campaigns were typically driven by top–down directives that dictated general statements of e-government goals and principles from the central Chinese government; municipal governments, which had different local situations and needs, customized municipal e-government strategies to anchor the generic e-government initiatives to their local reality. The Shanghai government, in particular, sought to tap these strategies to minimize inefficiency due to unsynergized e-government initiatives by different agencies, and to strengthen the municipality's position in China's transformation.

Background

At this time, Shanghai had implemented several specialized stand-alone information systems to automate back-office processes, and set up a basic online presence (www.shanghai.gov.cn). However, most of these initiatives were rudimentary. Thus, the Shanghai government aimed to push for more dynamic and interactive systems.

In 1998, eight agencies submitted separate proposals for smart cards to the Shanghai government, while various other agencies were contemplating issuing their own cards. The idea was thus mooted for a municipality-wide smart card rather than multiple cards, and the individual proposals were rejected. Instead, the Shanghai social security card project was born. This all-in-one smart card would record key personal information (e.g., name, identification number, fingerprint, medical insurance account number, housing fund account number, etc.), and enable citizens to access a wide variety of Government to Citizen (G2C) services. However, while the card's functionalities would extend beyond merely social security-related services, it was still called the social security card (see Table 1).

The Shanghai government also hoped that this e-government initiative would provide fresh new impetus to the municipality's economy and strengthen their position as a leader in China's transformation. As one informant noted:

"Shanghai is the commercial center of China. We hope to take the lead in the country-wide endeavor of digitization. We aim to draw further attention from the central government through showcasing our significant achievement. This will put us in an advantageous position in the competition for resources against other provinces and municipalities."

Table 1. Functionalities of the Shanghai Social Security Card

Service	Card Functionalities
Social security	• Registration of employment/unemployment status, application for unemployment insurance benefits, registration for vocational training (as part of unemployment insurance benefits) • Application for work-related injury assessment, application for work-related injury insurance benefits • Application for living subsidies, collection of living subsidies
Public security	• Cancellation and change of residential status
Civil administration	• Registration of marriage and divorce
Medical insurance	• Certification of retiree medical benefits • Management of medical insurance accounts
Housing fund	• Application for home loan
Others	• Application for driving license

Stage 1: Initiation (September 1998–December 2000)

On September 21, 1998, the Shanghai government laid out a three-year time frame for the social security card project. The project was championed by the Shanghai Municipal Informatization Commission, which reported directly to the vice mayor in charge of municipal development. The commission was empowered to coordinate the efforts of five other government agencies: The Shanghai Labor and Social Security Bureau, the Shanghai Municipal Bureau of Public Security, the Shanghai Municipal Bureau of Civil Affairs, the Shanghai Municipal Medical Insurance Bureau, and the Shanghai Municipal Public Health Bureau.

As a key government project, this initiative received personal attention from the mayor of Shanghai and was funded by the Shanghai Science and Technology Development Foundation. In addition, the Shanghai government established and empowered a project team to handle this initiative, partnered a chip maker and a research institute to develop the technological infrastructure, built a regulatory framework, and educated citizens to prepare for a smooth transition to a new service delivery mode.

In addition, this e-government project caught the attention of the Chinese central government. As they were seeking to further computerize China's social security system, China's Ministry of Labor and Social Security announced in September 1999 that they would collaborate with the Shanghai government in this area. This collaboration enabled the Shanghai government to leverage the intellectual and financial resources of the central government authority. As an informant noted:

> "Engaging and sustaining government attention is crucial for a mega-project like this one... Government support in the forms of financial resources and institutional endorsement makes the project move forward."

With municipal and central government support in place, the project team focused on streamlining back-office processes and exploring feasible technological solutions. The project champion initiated regular meetings with representatives from various agencies to discuss their operational processes and problems. Via this process, agreements were reached on several key issues, including the overall system design, plan for an administrative institution, design of the regulatory framework, and channels of information collection.

The project team was delegated authority by the Shanghai government to manage this initiative, and this helped the team to reduce the resistance to back-office process reengineering. This also helped ensure that the team had access to the resources and support of agencies at different levels throughout the Shanghai government. The project team thus translated the key agreements into actable directives, proposed solutions, and made action plans. Several rounds of brainstorming were then followed by review sessions, as the mayor and vice mayor, who were the project sponsors, sought to forge consensus among the various agencies to amend their back-office processes in line with the agreed-upon functionalities of the social security card.

The project team then relied heavily on local researchers and practitioners to formulate a technological solution for the social security card system. Specifically, with strong backing from the Shanghai municipal government, the team successfully formed partnerships with Shanghai Hua Hong (Group) Co. Ltd., which had undertaken one of the largest projects in China's electronics industry, and with Fudan University, one of China's top universities.

Consequently, several alternative designs were proposed to the Shanghai government, and one was selected — to build an integrated central system by seamlessly integrating major citizen service subsystems (see Figure 1). Via a connected central database and the Internet, the system would allow citizens to use smart cards for identification, to conduct enquiries, and to make payment at government service counters. Networked agency counters would enable service transactions involving multiple agencies to be conducted from one location (e.g., when a citizen updated their personal particulars at one government agency, the new information would be captured in the central database and made accessible to other agencies).

Given the scope and complexity of the proposed social security card project, the need for an administrative institution dedicated to managing the system became clear. The Shanghai social security card Service Center was thus set up in early 1999. Then, when the project scope expanded to include a citizen service information system in November

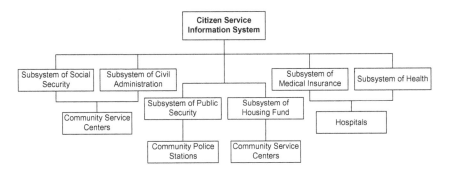

Figure 1. Major Citizen Service Subsystems under the Citizen Service Information Center.

2000, this organization was renamed the Shanghai Social Security and Citizen Service Information Center.

Stage 2: Dissemination (January 2001–December 2001)

To facilitate the dissemination process, in March 2001, the Shanghai Municipal Informatization Commission, the project champion, set up a subordinate organization — the Administrative Office of Shanghai Social Security and Citizen Service Information System — to oversee the project implementation. Following five months of preparation, this organization crafted two policies which laid down a set of guiding principles and practices as part of the legal and regulatory framework to guide project implementation: The "Administrative Method for Shanghai social security card," which spelled out the roles and responsibilities of the government and citizens in using the card, and the "Administrative Method for Shanghai Social Security and Citizen Service Information System," which detailed the roles and responsibilities of government agencies in charge of social security, civil administration, public security, housing fund, medical insurance, and electronic security.

The two policies were formally endorsed by the Shanghai government and took effect from August 2001. Thus, throughout the implementation, the municipal government would provide high-level guidance to resolve any disputes. Broad-based training would also be conducted among government agencies and hospitals, and for citizens. The project team would communicate with government staff primarily via internal documents and newsletters, which were circulated in a top–down manner from the municipal government to its 19 county-level government divisions, then to the 220 township-level government divisions, and finally to the 5,430 village-level government divisions. No effort was spared in reaching out to the public, as multiple channels of communication were employed. As one informant recalled:

> "We tried to introduce the new system to the public through TV, newspapers, banners at main streets and shopping centers, information booths at community centers, and a round-the-clock hotline. We tried to reach different user groups, and gain their trust and buy-in for the smart card system."

Moreover, considering the scope and impact of the system, the project team opted for an incremental approach during implementation (see Figure 2). The social security cards were first launched in nine districts of the central urban area. To ensure a smooth rollout of this large-scale initiative, the project team decided not to activate the card's medicare function at this time. This same approach was employed as implementation was subsequently expanded to the peripheral areas (i.e., the other 10 districts and one county). In addition, the project rollout was staggered among different user groups (i.e., retirees, Shanghai employees, and non-Shanghai employees) to give the project team adequate control and time for effective trial-and-error learning. For example, the initial rollout in the urban central districts was targeted at retirees.

At the same time, the administrative office held joint meetings with relevant agencies and private-sector experts to further adjust government back-office processes, modify regulatory guidelines, and fine-tune the technological architecture. All problems and solutions were also carefully documented. By the end of 2001, smart cards had been issued to the majority of the target population. Given the take-up rate of the new social security card, the magnetic cards that previously facilitated medicare account management, were subsequently abolished in March 2002.

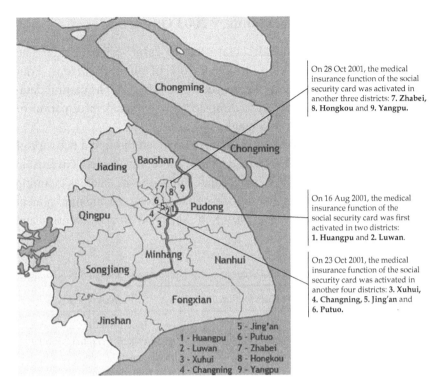

On 28 Oct 2001, the medical insurance function of the social security card was activated in another three districts: **7. Zhabei, 8. Hongkou and 9. Yangpu.**

On 16 Aug 2001, the medical insurance function of the social security card was first activated in two districts: **1. Huangpu and 2. Luwan.**

On 23 Oct 2001, the medical insurance function of the social security card was activated in another four districts: **3. Xuhui, 4. Changning, 5. Jing'an and 6. Putuo.**

Figure 2. Modular Implementation of System throughout Shanghai Municipality (Adapted from http://huayuindustries.com/images/map_shanghai_districts_gif.gif (last accessed: August 6, 2008)).

Concurrently, the technology provided, Shanghai Hua Hong (Group) Co. Ltd., committed a lot of resources during the implementation process. They set up a technical support team of experienced engineers and technicians. This team was organized into groups based on their areas of expertise (e.g., smart card technology, equipment maintenance, and system application). When about 4,000 machines were installed in 108 hospitals in the Huangpu and Luwan districts for system testing, team members took turns to be stationed at the hospitals, and worked round the clock to tackle system problems, circuit errors, and encryption issues. Shanghai Hua Hong also comprehensively documented all the knowledge gained over this process for future rollouts of the social security card and for their own product development.

Stage 3: Popularization (January 2003 Onwards)

By June 2005, the Shanghai social security card Service Center had issued over 9.3 million cards to about 70% of eligible citizens. Four types of social security cards were issued (see Table 2). The central database of the social security system hosted key personal information of about 20 million citizens in Shanghai.

A wide range of citizen services were provided through a network of 2,895 service centers all over Shanghai. The card enabled citizens in Shanghai to conduct social security-related transactions, such as claiming medical expenses, paying home loans, and applying for unemployment subsidies. The Administrative Office of Shanghai Social Security and

Table 2.   The Four Types of Social Security Cards Issued by the Shanghai Government.

Social Security Card	Cardholder	Functionality
	Blue Card Shanghai residents over 16 years old	Basic functionalities of social security card: Personal information management, identification, and information enquiry
	Red Card Senior Shanghai residents over 70 years old	Senior Shanghai residents entitlement to certain privileged services provided to senior citizens, and basic functionalities of the social security card
	Golden Card Retired officials in Shanghai	Identification of retired officials, entitlement to certain privileged services provided to retired officials and senior citizens, and basic functionalities of the social security card
	Green Card (Matriculation Card) Students below 16 years old in Shanghai	Student information management

Citizen Service Information System was also working with several major banks and technology providers, to study the feasibility of linking up this citizen database to banking systems to enable online payment for G2C services.

This project had several other repercussions. Their private sector partner, Shanghai Hua Hong, gained a foothold in government smart card technologies and won a few other contracts, such as the Shanghai public transportation Innovative Contracting (IC) project. In addition, various patents were filed, such as patents for a chop technology, POS machine, and a collection of 7,400 rare Chinese characters for the smart card database.

A key part of this stage was the replication of Shanghai's e-government implementation model in other Chinese municipalities and provinces. Several neighboring provinces thus entered into collaborative agreements with the Shanghai government to tap the knowledge and experiences that the latter had gleaned from this project. Unlike the top–down relationship between the central and municipal governments, the relationship between municipal governments was largely based on collaboration and reciprocity. Extended implementation also facilitated the continuous renewal and improvement of the e-government implementation model in response to changing environments.

Although it was still acknowledged that cultivating an e-government culture among all citizens was not a straightforward task, Shanghai's successful digitizing of their social security administration has since spread across China as a proven e-government model. In addition, the success of this project was of strategic importance to Shanghai, as the municipal government proactive participation in and significant advancement of China's key initiatives would put Shanghai a favorable position over other Chinese cities and provinces in future resource allocation from the central government.

Discussion Questions

1. Identify the main phases during the implementation of Shanghai's social security card system, and the key activities and players in each phase.
2. What are the advantages of adopting a modular approach to disseminate information during this e-government project? What are the challenges in

adopting modular information dissemination? What are the advantages of adopting a modular approach in the roll-out of Shanghai's social security card system? What are the challenges in adopting a modular roll-out? In your opinion, should this modular approach be employed in an e-government system implementation? Provide justifications for your stance.

3. What are the benefits of implementing a standard nationwide system? What are its disadvantages? What are the benefits of allowing each state to implement their own system? What are its disadvantages? In your opinion, which course of action is preferable? Why?

4. What is unique about implementing an e-government system in a developed country? What is unique about implementing an e-government system in a developing country?

Damai

Carmen Mei Ling Leong

Introduction

On November 5, 2011, Duan Dong Xu began work at Damai as its new CIO and was meeting the CEO and founder, Cao Jie, on the same day. From his new boss's office window, Duan could look out over the bustling morning crowd on Beijing Dongzhong Street, and he felt excited to have joined the largest online ticketing firm of China. From his encounter with Cao Jie during his job interview, Duan understood that Cao Jie intended to take the company to the next level, and Duan was eager to be part of that process. "I was running delivery services for e-commerce companies in 1998, and I saw an opportunity to go into the online ticketing business. Over the years, we have established our name in China's ticketing industry and are quite well known among customers," said Cao Jie, sitting in a high-backed black leather chair opposite Duan. Duan nodded in agreement. "I believe that the next thing we should pursue is to position Damai as a platform provider, just like eBay. I have always wanted to build a platform for our suppliers and agents so that they could interact directly with one another. I think this is the right time to do it." Duan understood that his new boss's aspiration was to expand the company by providing platform services because of its success in B2C business. This would enlarge the scope of Damai's business for future development. He recalled the concept of the "two-sided platform" from the MBA program he had recently completed. "I think what you have in mind is a two-sided platform. It enables direct interactions between multiple types of customers that are affiliated with an organization. In addition to eBay, there are other examples of platform providers, such as Alibaba, Amazon, and Google, thanks to the prevalence of information technology." From the smile on Cao Jie's face, Duan knew that he hit the nail on the head. He could not remember the details, but he remembered that there were challenges associated with the two-sided platform that were discussed in his MBA class. He noted these on his to-do list because he wanted to make sure that he incorporated them into his proposal. Of course, the first thing was to understand in detail the development of the company to-date. It would be important to leverage the company's strengths and capabilities. He recalled that several of his new colleagues had been with the company for years. He should catch up with them over lunch before the week ended.

Industry Background

China's ticketing industry has undergone rapid growth over the past decade. Since the advent of the widespread digital distribution of music, music record labels have reported a considerable decline in sales. This turmoil in the music industry has caused record companies and artists worldwide to rely on live performance as their main source of revenue, which resulted in an abundance of performances and concerts. Simultaneously, the Chinese government was refining its cultural and entertainment industry. After the 16th Communist Party of China (CPC) National Congress in 2002, the government launched a series of initiatives to bring formerly government-affiliated agencies, including film studios and TV stations, to the market with the aim of stimulating the consumption of cultural and entertainment products. This favourable environment, coupled with China's growing GDP and rising standard of living — China's per capita income surpassed US$5,000 in 2011 — contributed to an expansion in cultural and entertainment spending that reached 1 trillion RMB (US$161 billion) in 2011. This encouraged the development of the

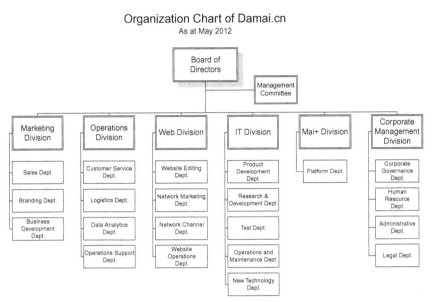

Figure 1.　China's Ticketing Market 2011 (The ticketing industry excludes transportation tickets, such as air tickets and train tickets).

Note: Dept — Department
Source: Enfogrowth 2012.

ticketing industry in China, which reached 166 billion RMB (US$27 billion) in the same year. Figure 1 shows various categories of tickets and the market share breakdown.

The new government policy and market evolution helped create changes in the value chain of China's ticketing industry. Before this, event organizers handled the design, production, sales, and distribution of tickets. Because they generated the tickets, they were also recognized as the *suppliers* in the ticketing industry. These tickets were then sold through venue operators with whom the event organizers worked, which meant that a customer had to purchase a ticket at a theater, art center, stadium, or theme park. In some instances, venue operators were also considered to be suppliers when they organized events such as crosstalks (traditional Chinese comedic performances, usually with two performers) and theatrical presentations. Since 2002, new roles gradually emerged in the industry. As the industry matured, ticketing *distributors* emerged as the mediators between event organizers and customers; such distributors offered a new channel through which customers could obtain tickets. Distributors operated as independent entities and owned networks of ticket-selling points — such as counters — at various locations. The distributors progressively took over the task of designing, producing, selling, and distributing tickets from event organizers. In addition, distributors worked with ticketing *agents*. Agents played a simpler role than distributors — they were re-sellers of tickets situated between distributors and customers — and were important for distributors in expanding coverage areas. Because of their limited capacity, agents seldom approached suppliers directly. For large-scale events, such as concerts, suppliers would grant exclusive rights to a distributor who would then work with a group of agents.

Online ticketing was introduced to China with the advent of the Internet. In the early 2000s, online ticketing was stymied by various institutional deficiencies in China, including poor infrastructure, immature online payment systems, unreliable delivery services, and an inefficient regulatory system. Other than in the few major cities, the IT literacy of customers was low. It was challenging to entice customers to pay a "faceless" vendor before goods arrived. To make things worse, China was plagued with ticketing fraud even before the advent of the Internet; when tickets were offered online, these same con artists utilized the Internet as a tool for ticketing fraud, which reduced confidence in online purchasing even more. However, despite the difficulties at its inception, online ticketing began to gain a foothold in the mid-2000s, as e-commerce matured. By March 2011, as China overcame its binding constraints and became the world's largest e-commerce market, Damai, China's largest online ticketing firm, had issued more than 10 million tickets.

Organizational Background

By 1998, IT entrepreneurs in China had jumped onto the bandwagon of electronic commerce. However, because of capital limitations, Cao Jie, the founder of Damai, doubted that he could start an e-commerce company. He conducted market research and found that 90% of e-commerce operations in the US were conducted by express delivery companies. With all his savings, he established a company in 1998 that offered delivery services. When he served a few e-commerce players, he experienced a sudden surge in the demand for his delivery services in one particular area, tickets to "Rhinoceros in Love", a classic drama of modern Chinese theater. Cao Jie noticed a great business opportunity. It would cost him almost nothing to sell the performance tickets. If he could strike a deal with performance organizers, he could sell tickets "on behalf of them" and remaining tickets would be returned to the organizers. Conversely, the organizers should be happy that they could "outsource" ticket sales and delivery. He believed that the logistics capability of his company would be his main selling point. After a few rounds of negotiations, his idea was turned into a reality. With that, piao.com.cn was born in 1999 as a web portal selling tickets for the first time on behalf of a Russian circus. The marketing campaign by the performance organizer popularized piao.com.cn, which was later reincarnated into Damai (a homophone for "best-selling" in Chinese).

In the beginning, customers visited the company's web portal to place an order for tickets. Damai staff would then contact the customers on the telephone to confirm orders. After gathering the orders, the company would send someone to the ticket-selling points (often at the venue in which the performance was held) to purchase tickets. When the ticket was delivered to the customer, payment was made and the transaction was complete. At that time, ticket design and production were handled by the event organizers and all tickets were pre-printed. If there were printing errors, tickets had to be reprinted and this could cause disruptions in ticket distribution. However, the situation was considerably improved when Damai took over the production of tickets from suppliers in 2005. A ticketing system was developed in-house for online purchases. Later, the company was also put in charge of the marketing and after-sales tasks, such as ticket verification and admission control.

Within five years, Damai had become the leading online ticketing firm in China and enjoyed a 70% market share that was approximately three times that of its closest rivals (ZhongYan and YongLe). Currently, it had 35 branches in the largest cities in China, a staff of approximately 600 and a distribution network of 20,000 agents nationwide. Figure 2 shows the business network of Damai and the types of suppliers and agents in its network. In addition to musical and cultural events, Damai sold tickets for sports, movie, entertainment, and travel sector events. As of the end of 2011, the company had approximately 8 million registered users. As of March 2011,

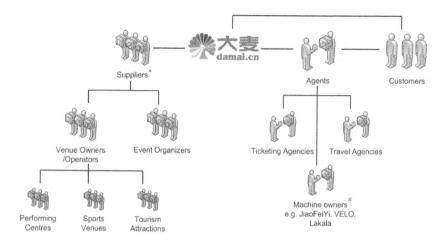

 Suppliers were ticket generators who sought distributor's (and sometimes agent's) service to sell tickets.

 Machine owners were ticketing agents who sold the tickets through their own network of machines/terminals at different locations.

JiaoFeiYi was the operator of third-party payment terminals that were deployed at various locations such as office buildings, neighborhoods, banks, campuses, supermarkets, etc.;

Lakala was the operator of personal payment terminals that were placed at home for ease of various payments, such as utility bills and credit cards;

VELO was the owner of interactive advertising terminals that were widely deployed at the rapid transit stations.

Figure 2.   Damai's Business Network.

it had been involved in more than 10,000 events that amounted to approximately 10 million tickets being printed. Organizers of major events such as 2008 pre-Olympic test events and NBA China Games had chosen Damai as their exclusive distributor. Its exceptional performance attracted investment from Lenovo in 2004. Furthermore, Ticketmaster — the US-based ticketing company that was the world's largest — has offered to acquire Damai, although it was rejected by Cao Jie more than once.

Development of Damai

Selling Tickets Directly to Customers

At the cafeteria, Duan was speaking to a few experienced staff members from different divisions. They had long heard about the CEO's plan and were glad that Duan had joined them and spearheaded such initiatives. Chen, the Senior Manager of Business Development Department, Marketing Division, said:

"In the early days, ticket selling occurred over ticket counters. It was inconvenient and frustrating when there was an overwhelming response to the performances or events. Traditional transactions were limited to an allocated time at specific spots, but an online website could enable purchasing anytime and anywhere. When Damai was first incorporated in 1999, the company launched a simple website that allowed customers to 'order' a ticket online. A paper-based ticket would then be delivered to the customer's doorstep. Later, we launched an online purchasing portal in 2004. Customers completed the payment online and they could later collect a ticket from our agencies or do a self-printing at Damai's terminals."

The most critical issue in encouraging online ticketing was to enhance customer's confidence in Damai's fraud prevention measures. Considerable efforts have been dedicated to prevent counterfeit tickets and to educate customers. One way to achieve this was through the implementation of multiple security measures with respect to the tickets. There were at least six anti-counterfeiting features on its tickets, such as 2D barcode, which made it difficult to imitate (Figure 3). Damai also worked with venue operators by providing them verification devices (Figure 4) as part of admission control. Moreover, customers were able to verify their tickets by entering a verification code in the online authentication system (Figure 5), which was also available in a mobile version. Customers were encouraged to report ticketing fraud incidents through their website to alert other customers. In addition, Damai committed to ensure the safety of customer's information and was certified compliant with international security standards in 2011. Over time, this strengthened the reputation of Damai as a trustworthy source of tickets.

Simultaneously, Damai prepared for the launch of electronic ticketing and other service-enhancing online features such as online seat selection. In addition to reducing operating costs, these features refined the customer's experience in purchasing tickets. In the past, customers were not allowed to select a seat when they purchased online; Damai was the first

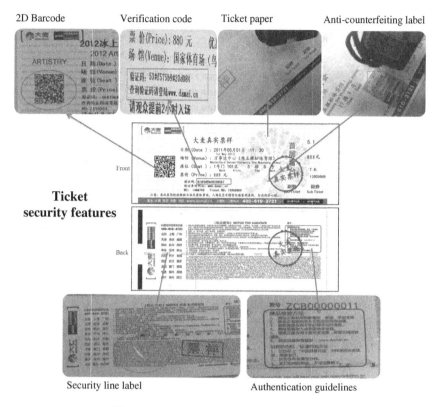

Figure 3. Damai's Ticket Security Features.

to launch the program that enabled seat selection. As the Director of IT Division recalled:

> "Damai became more famous in China's ticketing industry in 2009 regarding a concert from Li Yuchun (a famous pop singer of China). Within 24 hours, all the tickets were sold as we launched e-tickets and online seat selections. The ardent fans grabbed all the seats in a day. This was a new experience for them because the entire process was transparent — you were able to see how many tickets are available. As long as you were fast, you could obtain a ticket. This was a fair process."

Damai realized that customer visits to their website were driven purely for functional purposes, which simply means that customers came

Deployment of ticket verification devices at
Wukesong Indoor Stadium (capacity: 18,000 pax)   Ticket verification devices

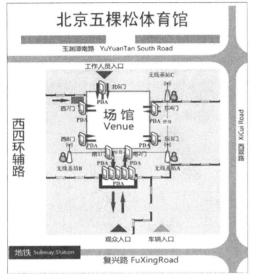

Figure 4.   The Deployment of Ticket Verification Devices.

Enter the verification
code here to check the
ticket authenticity

Figure 5.   Damai's Online Ticket Authentication System.

to the website only to purchase a ticket. This could be a risk if competitors
caught up with Damai in the provision of services, pricing, or IT capability because customers would have no incentive to stay with Damai. Thus,
Damai strove to increase the number of informal visits that customers

Categories of interest (e.g., Concert, Musical, Theater,
Dance, Sports, Travel, Parenting, Movie)

Figure 6.   Damai's B2C Website Home Page.

would make to the website. First, an analysis was conducted to understand
a customer's favorite events. To attract customers, the website was
categorized into several major groups such as rock music, drama, classics,
kids and family (Figure 6). For each group, an interactive sharing forum
was provided that facilitated communications among customers with
similar interests. In addition to the in-group discussions, customers are
able to "talk" to Damai through various channels such as feedback and
polling — polling allowed customers to vote for the performances that
they wished for. This fulfilled other social requirements of the customers,
as the Director of IT Division indicated:

> "The consumption of cultural and entertainment product is driven by stimu-
> lus. By providing peripheral services, we are part of the stimulus also. For
> example, because we provide the social network platform, customers are
> encouraged to make friends as they purchase their tickets. In other words,
> we are fulfilling other aspects of customer needs in addition to simply
> providing tickets."

Along with a proliferation of social media, Damai has been busy working on its strategy for "weibo", a Chinese Twitter-like microblog. Since the end of 2010, they have created approximately 1000 accounts, posting messages about events and artists and interacting with customers to create a mass of "followers". Figure 7 shows a screenshot of Damai's weibo (left). This encouraged customers to socialize amongst themselves and promoted information dissemination. On average, Damai attracted approximately 3 million customer visits to its weibo every month. The Assistant Director of Web Division explained:

> "In the past, customers have had no further relationship with Damai after they finished purchasing tickets. However, as we launch various initiatives in weibo, a connection can be maintained. For example, they can share a photo of the concert when they are at the scene. In addition, customers can use mobile phone positioning to locate a friend at the venue."

Smartphones offered a new avenue to engage customers. Damai launched the mobile version of its B2C website (Figure 7 middle), which offered an almost "ubiquitous" channel to the customers. With the mobile version, customers could make a purchase and socialize on Damai's social network platform anytime and anywhere, without being tethered to a computer. To further improve the ease of purchase, Damai used existing resources, such as posters. New posters now come with a 2D barcode, which customers could scan and purchase almost immediately, as shown in Figure 7 (right).

In addition, Damai turned the bulk of its customers into a "resource." The group-buy feature was incorporated to encourage customers to pull others along to enjoy a discount off the ticket price. Moreover, they could share accommodation and transportation fees when travelling to the venue, as the Assistant Director of Web Division explained:

> "We were thinking from a more interactive perspective. We considered the functions that customers would require when they bought a ticket. This function of "yiqipin" (which meant "fight together" in Chinese) allows customers to buy tickets together (for a discount) and to share accommodation and transportation if they must travel to another city for the performance... Customers can take the initiative to obtain others' responses ... and they feel a value-added service from these little functions."

| Damai's weibo | Damai's mobile site | Poster with 2D barcode |

Figure 7.   Damai's Mobile and Social Network Environment.

Selling Tickets Indirectly Through Agents

"Although our companies have a presence in more than 30 cities, we are definitely not able to cater to everyone's needs at some second- and third-tier cities... The online portal provides only one channel and we want to ensure that we are accessible conveniently, even for customers with no Internet connection ..."

— Assistant Director of IT Division

The above statement explained the reasons why Damai continued to work with approximately 20,000 distribution agents to provide flexibility and convenience in purchasing tickets from Damai. As Damai set up branches in large cities, they also established partnerships with smaller agents to expand service coverage. As shown in Figure 1, certain agents include ticketing agencies, travel agencies, and terminal operators such as JiaoFeiYi, Lakala, and VELO. In large cities, these partnerships served to construct a pervasive network of Damai's service; in smaller cities, more-over, the collaborations helped Damai to penetrate local markets efficiently.

Partnerships with agents relied on an effective exchange of information. In addition to the number of agents and geographical distances, the major challenge facing Damai was differences in established operations and practices. For those agents from the ticketing industry, such as ticketing agencies and travel agencies, the collaborations may differ across cities and with individual agents in terms of agent fee structures, charging procedures, authorization processes, and partnering models. For instance, different agent fees might apply to partnerships with agents from Chengdu compared to agents from Beijing because of the city tiers. Conversely, with regard to agents from other industries such as VELO, they were accustomed to a business operation that was vastly different from Damai. Faced with the diversity of its agents, Damai required an IT system that could link all its agents to its B2C engine. In developing this system, the Senior Manager (Damai) from IT Division (Product Development) pinpointed the basic requirement of the system:

> "The agents are located in different tiers of cities with diverse requirements for partnership. Additionally, the operating procedures differ across agents. We must ensure that our system satisfies the adaptability and flexibility demanded of distribution channel exploration at a nationwide level..."

The distribution system, *youpiaotong*, was developed by Damai's in-house IT team. It was provided to the ticketing agencies in the form of a computer and printer. As soon as the IT team installed the computer at agencies' workplace, they were able to access the backend database of Damai and start selling available tickets. In addition to this, the system was installed in the self-purchasing terminals of Damai. These terminals, in turn, were deployed at venues of agents such as convenience stores, schools, hotels, and venue owners. User-friendliness was a critical consideration to ensure that agents experienced a small learning curve with minimal disruption to their core businesses. Lastly, for agents who previously had their own terminals deployed at various locations (e.g., JiaoFeiYi, Lakala, and VELO), the *youpiaotong* system could be installed in existing machines, leveraging the network that they had previously built. Figure 8 shows the different terminals owned by agents. As the Senior Project Manager of the Business Development Department of the Marketing Division recalled, the distribution systems were critical in forming Damai's nationwide distribution network:

> "We used to have only dozens of small ticketing agencies in Beijing, but our sales channel department has extended our network. We have a wider coverage, and this would not be possible without our distribution system."

JiaoFeiYi: Lakala: VELO:
3rd-party bill payment   Personal bill payment   Interactive advertising
terminal   terminal   terminal

Figure 8.   Terminals Owned by Different Agents.

These systems alone did not, however, bring about the attachment that Damai wished to promote in its relationships with agents. Unlike a typical principal-agency relationship, Damai did not plan to commercially exploit its superior position in its connections to ticket suppliers. For instance, they could earn from the difference in commission that they received from suppliers and the commission that they distributed to agents. However, Damai was prepared to share profits with agents to sustain the relationship and grow the agent's coverage, which would eventually complement and expand Damai's sphere of influence in the industry. This message from the CEO was clear to all staff, as repeated by the Senior Manager (Damai) from the IT Division (Product Development):

> "We must promote our services and brand. Profit sharing with our agents is necessary. In fact, we are trying to expand our coverage by doing that."

This was implemented through a fair and transparent operation visible in the *youpiaotong* system. As Damai was selling tickets through its B2C website, it allowed its agents to access the identical pool of tickets. Moreover, they adopted a flat structure in their commission sharing with agents — whatever commission was offered by the supplier would be visible in the system. In other words, this meant that agents were enjoying the same commission rate as Damai.

> "We hope this increases our agents' competitive advantage. Being smaller, they often give discounts to attract customers... We ensure that this is visible in our system."
>
> — Channel Development Manager, Marketing Division (Channel Development Department)

As the working relationship grew over time, it revealed the complementary resources that both collaborating parties could offer. Often, these complementary resources could create synergy within inter-organizational partnerships. For instance, in the partnership with Lakala, Damai could leverage its marketing capabilities. Lakala, conversely, could make use of Damai resources in offering tickets. This has culminated in several marketing events organized jointly by Damai and Lakala. Through such events, they have explored additional ways to exchange resources between organizations. An example given by the Senior Manager from IT Division (Product Development) was the trading of tickets in exchange for advertising time:

> "With a close relationship with VELO and Lakala, we are able to exchange resources easily. We exchange tickets for advertising time... We have also organized several promotional events jointly. We sponsor tickets as prizes and Lakala helps us to promote Damai's brand."

Damai also worked closely with Sina, the parent company of Sina weibo, which had over 10 million user visits everyday. This mass of people has certainly attracted the attention of Damai, as mentioned by the Director (Social Media), IT Division (Research & Development):

> "Weibo has a huge user base, and they hope to introduce more services to their customers. There is definitely space for joint efforts [between Damai and Sina]."

The joint development effort between Damai and Sina materialized as a ticketing channel built by the parties. As the Senior Manager (Damai) from IT Division (Product Development) explained:

"If the user comes across the information about a ticket or an event on the Sina website, he/she can purchase it directly from Damai without leaving Sina's portal. Indirectly, Sina has become part of our B2C chain."

The Next Stage

Apart from enhancing the downstream process of distributing the tickets, Damai has dedicated much of its efforts toward enhancing its relationships with suppliers over the past three years. They offered marketing solutions as a value-added service to suppliers. Based on their experience, they advised suppliers about suitable venues for their events and the right advertising channels to reach their target audiences. In addition to ticket design, Damai has been involved in the design of marketing materials, such as posters and online flyers. They worked closely with suppliers in devising and implementing the online and offline marketing strategies for events, operating as part of the suppliers' marketing team. This has proven to be a particularly valuable service for overseas suppliers who were not familiar with the Chinese market.

However, the development of the ticketing industry in China was closely tied to regional factors. In first-tier cities such as Beijing, Shanghai, and Guangzhou, which are concentrated with huge entertainment venues, large-scale events were held, attracting audiences from all over China. Conversely, there were local markets in the provinces in which venue operators served mainly their local populations with smaller-scale cultural and entertaining performances such as crosstalks in Tianjin. Ticketing agents from these locations were therefore more familiar with the local environment and market conditions than Damai, who might only have had a branch of three to five staff members in the city. These agents enjoyed high levels of recognition among local customers and venue operators. With the growing emergence of these second- and third-tier cities, suppliers became increasingly interested in approaching these local agents directly in the cities in which the suppliers would like to hold events. Here, Damai faced difficulties in intercepting the direct dialog between suppliers and local agents.

Duan understood from his colleagues that Damai had a strong foundation in the B2C arena. Nonetheless, if it was complacent with their success in B2C, Damai might lose its leading position when the local agents caught up in the competition. Although no one in China's ticketing industry had initiated a B2B operation, he thought he could draw on the lessons from B2B players in other sectors. In ticketing, B2B would mean enabling direct transactions between suppliers of tickets and agents or even other distributors. He believed that his team would have no issues in designing the technological platform; the challenge involved the implementation and sustainment of this two-sided online platform as the company continued its B2C business. In other words, as Damai bridged the gap between suppliers and agents, it might lose its advantageous position as a ticket distributor who was the intermediary between the two. Moreover, how could he create value that was not as easy to imitate as the technology platform? He needed to highlight these issues and propose his solutions.

Reference

Enfogrowth. 2012 Development and Trends of China's Online Ticketing Industry. (available online at http://wenku.baidu.com/view/174c9ad13186bceb19e8bb95. html, 3 August 2012).

Discussion Questions

1. How is the two-sided online platform different from the current operating models of Damai?
2. Do you agree with Damai's CEO idea about the potential of the two-sided online platform in advancing the company? How would you evaluate the new e-business strategy?
3. What are the key challenges in implementing the two-sided online platform? If you are Mr. Duan, how would you propose to resolve these challenges?
4. What are some of the lessons learned from the previous success of Damai that can be replicated in the implementation process of its two-sided online platform?

10

Chang Chun Petrochemicals

Barney Tan and Tzu-Chuan Chou

Organizational Background

Chang Chun Petrochemicals (CCP) is the oldest petrochemical firm in Taiwan. It started as Chang Chun Plastics Co in 1949 for the purpose of manufacturing a form of engineering plastic known as the Phenolic Molding Compound. Over the years, CCP gradually increased the variety of its product offerings and expanded its production facilities to meet the increasing demands of the global market as its business grew exponentially through joint ventures and technology licensing. Today, CCP is an international company that provides a broad range of products from engineering plastics and electronic chemicals to molding materials. CCP owns more than 10 subsidies, with Chang Chun Petrochemical Co, Chang Chun Plastics Co., and Dairen Corporate being the three major ones. By 2007, CCP had successfully built business relationships with more than 15,000 customers located in 111 countries and offered more than 100 categories of products. It currently has more than 4,500 employees worldwide and an annual revenue of about US$4.6 billion, making it the one of the largest privately owned petrochemical firms in the country.

CCP's IT department was formed in 1984, marking the organization's first foray into the use of IT. Since its inception, the IT department has been instrumental in the deployment of IT projects at CCP, providing the driving force that propelled the organization through three major phases of systems implementation since 2001. The phases are internally abbreviated as the 'E-Phase' (E for Electronic), the 'M-Phase' (M for Mobile), and the 'U-Phase' (U for Ubiquitous) respectively. With just over 20 employees, the department has developed an internal reputation for its efficiency and ability to deliver business-critical IT systems that support the operations of the entire firm despite limited resources. The department is led by the organization's Senior Executive Vice President, who personally initiated and managed many instances of IT innovations at CCP.

The process and implementation of organizational improvization of CCP can be focused into four pertinent themes: (1) Development of the means for improvization, (2) detecting and interpreting triggers of organizational improvization, (3) the enactment of improvization, and (4) outcomes of organizational improvization centered on the facilitation of agile IT adoption and enterprise agility. In addition, CCP underwent three major phases of systems implementation as follows:

E-Phase (2001–2004)

From the establishment of the IT department in 1984 and prior to 2001, CCP's operations were supported by a DOS-based legacy system that was developed internally. In 2001, when Microsoft announced the launch of Windows XP, the DOS-based system was rendered obsolete, triggering the need for the implementation of a new system. Yet, the management of CCP was unwilling to commit the funds for an off-the-shelf ERP package (which costs between NT$30–100 million). Faced with a pressing need for a new system and yet constrained by the limited resources they had, the IT department was forced to improvize to deliver a solution. An in-house ERP development project was eventually launched with two overarching objectives: (1) Developing an ERP system to meet the present needs of CCP, which is, at the same time, scalable to support the future growth of the firm, and (2) implementing it at a lower cost than commercial, "off-the-shelf" packages.

Comprised of slightly over than 10 employees with limited knowledge about ERP systems and little prior experience in large-scale systems implementation, the IT department spent almost one year in implementing the system. During this period, the extensive business domain knowledge of the members of the IT department, accrued from the years of managing the DOS-based system, the unwavering support and the experimental environment encouraged by the top management, and a supportive culture marked by a fervent "can-do" spirit were critical to the success of systems implementation. Moreover, to augment their software development capabilities, CCP also engaged Lian Quan, a small software company with formidable research and technical capabilities, as their technical partner. The CASE (Computer Assisted Software Engineering) tools provided by Lian Quan played a critical role in simplifying the coding process for the internally developed system by enabling a consistent coding standard. The result was the successful implementation of an ERP system that was developed at a low cost (as compared to commercial ERP packages), within a short time frame (as compared to industry standards), and provided tailored support for the operations of the CCP. The means, triggers, process, and outcomes of improvization in IT deployment at CCP in the E-Phase are summarized in Table 1.

M-Phase (2005–2006)

The M-Phase of CCP's systems implementation journey was triggered by a construction accident in 2005. Prior to the accident, CCP was reliant on phone lines and ADSL for data transmission. However, these lines were severed in the construction accident and consequently, access to CCP's ERP system was down for several hours. Critical operational information could not be transmitted in time, which resulted in losses of over tens of millions of dollars because of the accident. At the same time, internal organizational stakeholders began to demand for remote access to some of CCP's IT applications. These driving forces, coupled with the opportunity provided by the emerging mobile technologies (i.e., 3G and Wi-Fi) provided the impetus to enable CCP's IT applications on the mobile platform. Yet, as the organizational resources allocated for the implementation of the M-Phase was similarly limited, and because the mobile applications market

Table 1.   Development and Leverage of the Capability for Improvization in IT Deployment in the E-Phase

---

Means for improvization

Extensive domain knowledge	*"A unique characteristic of our department is that staff turnover rate is very low. So many of our staff have extensive knowledge of the business processes because they have been supporting the operations of the organization since the DOS days... Being familiar with all the business process flows, all we had to do is to write it into the new system."*
	— Head of IT Department
Support from the top management, encouraging experimentation and tolerance for failure	*"The credit goes to our Senior Executive Vice President. He encourages and supports innovation without reservation. He is willing to let us try and experiment. Sometimes it is hard to justify an IT system's value if you purely look at the economic ROI. However, our boss is willing to invest in such 'high cost — low return' projects because he believes in the importance of giving employees the exposure to advanced technologies; technologies that he believes will be the trend of the future even though they are not yet widely adopted today. As a result, we, as IT staff, are less concerned about possibility of failure."*
	— Head of IT Department
Intrinsic motivation, supportive culture	*"We have a 'can do' spirit that originated from the time when we first started building our own ERP system. Throughout the entire process of starting from scratch to what we have achieved today, this spirit is continuously cultivated. Therefore, when we are faced with another IT challenge or opportunity today, we are much more confident (in handling the challenge or seizing the opportunity). It just does not seem to be that hard anymore."*
	— Deputy Head of IT Department

Triggers of improvization

Technology obsolescence	*"The new (Windows XP) will not support our DOS-based systems... It was a natural choice under the changing technological environment... We simply couldn't rely on simulating the DOS environment in Windows XP. It would cause a lot of trouble and big problems will emerge in the future."*
	— Sector Supervisor of IT Department

(*Continued*)

Table 1. (*Continued*)

Professional interactions	*"Even before Microsoft announced the details of (Windows XP) ... (From our interactions with external IT communities-of-practice) we learnt that our DOS system will probably not be supported... We reacted to it quickly. We realized we couldn't continue relying on DOS, so we decided to switch to Windows."* — IT Project Team Leader

Enactment of improvization

Bricolage of creativity and technical skills	*"We studied several ERP vendors' products, took their strong points and used that in the design of our own system. Based on what we saw, we made guesses on their underlying architecture design and discussed among ourselves how we could restructure and redesign them (to make them better)."* — Senior IT Executive A
Acquisition of technology/ system development capabilities	*"Our information on the latest technologies is very limited. So we need to rely on these small companies (technology partners like Lian Quan) to gather such information and present them to us because they are out there in the field..."* — Senior Executive Vice President *"We used the CASE tools (provided by Lian Quan) extensively. With the CASE tools, the process of software development is simplified. Technical skills became less important to software development. Understanding the process flows were more important."* — Head of IT Department

Improvizational outcomes

Rapid, more cost-efficient mode of systems implementation	*"The cost of off-the-shelf ERP packages (for a company of our scale) ranges from NT$30 million to more than NT$100 million. We spent NT$12 million in developing our own... In terms of time spent, one of our factories in Changshu adopted SAP's ERP system and took 3 years, while we only took 1 year for an organization-wide scale project."* — Head of IT Department
Effective support for business operations	*"Our IT systems are designed to cater to our users' needs and match their habits. Sometimes it is hard to change the users' habit, so we decided to design our system to match their requirements so as to lower their resistance. From the IT department's standpoint, a huge advantage is the flexibility in customizing the system based on user feedback. We don't have to engage external consultants again and again, and ask if they can make certain changes. We will just do it ourselves."* — Deputy Head of IT Department

lacked the specific applications that CCP needed, the IT department was once again forced to improvize to develop the solution they needed.

In the implementation of the M-Phase, the IT infrastructure developed in the E-Phase, the capabilities for coordination and teamwork developed between the various business units and the IT department over time, and a powerful intrinsic motivation driven by a stoic, collective sense of mission, were prior resources that were crucial to the success of IT deployment. In addition, the IT department relied heavily on their existing technical expertise, developed from the experience of the E-Phase, and acquired complementary technological resources in the form of pre-written software modules to make improvization possible. The result was the successful launch of a comprehensive suite of mobile applications; including a Push Mail, an M-ERP, an M-CRM, and a remote facility monitoring application, that was once again developed in a fast and cost-efficient manner. In addition, as compared to existing off-the-shelf alternatives, the internally developed system had more functionality and represented a better fit with the business processes of CCP. Table 2 provides a summary of the means, triggers, process, and outcomes of improvization in IT deployment at CCP in the M-Phase.

U-Phase (2007–Present)

The major systems implemented in the U-Phase were triggered by a number of changes in the external and internal organizational environment in 2007. In the case of the GPS vehicle tracking system, the impetus for systems implementation came about as a result of a legislative change in Taiwan that required all vehicles transporting hazardous materials to be outfitted with a tracking device for safety reasons. In the case of the QR-Code-enabled inventory and logistics management system and the IP-PBX telephone system, they were implemented as a result of a directive from CCP's Senior Executive Vice President. By this phase, the IT department had become conditioned to working with resource constraints and an improvizational mode of IT deployment. Consequently, even when they were given the option to purchase an expensive "off-the-shelf" solution in the case of the IP-PBX telephone system, they chose to improvize to "piece together" their own solution instead.

Table 2.   Development and Leverage of the Capability for Improvization in IT Deployment in the M-Phase

Means for improvization

Leveraging existing IT infrastructure	*"The underlying ERP system (developed in the E-Phase) provides the foundation for the M-Phase... Let's say that a manager wants to access an application on his mobile phone ... the mobile phone is just the platform right? There has to be a backend system ... that is our ERP. Without our ERP, all the applications that we wanted to develop would have been impossible."* — IT Department Head
Collaboration and social relationships	*"During the E-Phase, we established a number of cross-functional steering committees consisting of the managers of the various departments to chart the direction of systems development. By the time of the M-Phase, as we interact and become more familiar with one another over time, our coordination improved. We had a better understanding of each other's business processes and we had no qualms about raising our requirements to the IT department... Between the different departments, we also looked at the different ways in which we can collaborate to make the overall operations (of CCP) more efficient."* — Business Process Owner
Intrinsic motivation for improvization	*"We didn't get any material rewards for our success in the previous phase but we are happy to do it... In spite of our limited resources, we see delivering solutions (to organizational problems) as part of our job scope, part of our responsibilities. I think the culture ... a culture for innovation ... really crystallized after the E-Phase. We were more confident of our abilities and we were given the freedom to be creative."* — Head of IT Department

Triggers of improvization

Business crisis	*"Our daily revenue is tens of millions of dollars. Even if our ERP is just down for an hour, the economic loss would be catastrophic. In Miao Li (one of CCP's production bases), after only a few minutes of systems breakdown, the line of trucks (waiting to be loaded) stretched all the way from the summit (where the facility was based) to the foot of the hill. There were 2 miles of trucks."* — Head of IT Department

(*Continued*)

Table 2.   (*Continued*)

Business needs	*"The managers of the various business units and the top management asked for (applications on the mobile platform)... Particularly for push mail because checking emails is really a very important part of their work... It was a good timing. At that time, 3G just came out. It solved a huge performance issue that previous mobile platforms couldn't solve. 3G made M-ERP (and other mobile applications) possible."*
	— Deputy Head of IT Department
Monitoring the technological landscape	*"We had been monitoring mobile technologies for some time... At our organization, a few staff members are dedicated to monitoring the developments in the technological landscape... One (staff member) is responsible for monitoring web application frameworks ... we have another four looking at mobile platforms and applications."*
	— Head of IT Department

Enactment of improvization

Bricolage of technical expertise	*"Once you know how to do it, it (systems implementation) can be very fast. However, if you do not know how to do it, it will take you forever. I think by the time (of the M-phase), we have reached a certain level of technical competency, implementing the initiatives of this phase were much easier (as compared to the E-phase)."*
	— Head of IT Department
Acquisition of technological resources	*"Although there were very few mobile apps that met our needs, we bought whatever (apps) that was compatible and modified them according to our needs. I think it is important to 'stand on the shoulder of giants'... as long as someone has written something that we need (and if it is priced reasonably), we would buy them... Given the time and (resource constraints) that we had, we can't be writing all our apps by ourselves!"*
	— IT Project Team Leader

(*Continued*)

Table 2.   (*Continued*)

Improvizational Outcomes

Faster, cost-efficient systems implementation	*"At the time, it will cost a several hundred thousand (NT$) dollars just for a simple mobile scanning inventory output system that can run on a PDA. And with all the applications we wanted, it will take the vendor half a year to deploy. We did everything ourselves... It is much faster, cheaper and easier to control."*

— Senior IT Executive B

Effective support for business operations	*"With the M-CRM, managers can access the information they need anywhere, anytime... With our inventory management applications on the mobile platform, the efficiency of inventory and logistics management is also greatly enhanced... (As compared to commercial, off-the-shelf solutions), we found a company doing a software called 'mobile intelligence', but its functionality was very limited and incompatible with our existing processes. We have much better control (over the functionalities of our system) in this way."*

— Head of IT Department

In the implementation of the three major systems of the U-Phase, the existing hardware, software, and network infrastructure, the cohesion between the IT department and the various business units that crystallized over a long history of collaboration, and the creativity of the IT department, were previously developed capabilities that facilitated the success of IT deployment. Moreover, the IT department leveraged their technical proficiency to experiment with various alternative solutions concurrently in iterative cycles of planning and execution. Finally, similar to the earlier phases, the outcome of improvization was cost savings and the successful launches of a number of IT systems that permeated, supported, and enhanced many interrelated aspects of CCP's operations. A summary of the means, triggers, process and outcomes of improvization in IT deployment at CCP in the U-Phase is provided in Table 3.

Table 3.   Development and Leverage of the Capability for Improvization in IT Deployment in the U-Phase

Means for improvization	
Foundational IT Infrastructure	*"To link all the various new systems and our existing ones, we relied on our existing network infrastructure… In terms of the hardware that supported our new applications, most of the infrastructure is already there… For the software of our new systems, the only difference was that we used a different development environment… We used Visual Studio to develop our new systems…"* — Senior IT Executive B
Collaboration with business units for domain knowledge	*"When we were implementing our QR-Code inventory management system, we were actively consulting with the various factories and business units. We told them what QR-Code could do … they would imagine how it can be applied to their business processes and tell us what kind of support they hope to receive using the technology… We would then implement the relevant modules based on their specifications."* — Senior IT Executive C
Creativity	*"I think over time, we have learnt how to be creative to deal with 'surprises' (like the directive to implement QR-Code)… Otherwise, we would not be able to come up with the solutions that the top management wants all the time. (The top management) would throw us an idea … an abstract concept … On one hand, it indicates that the top management has a lot of confidence in us… (On the other,) we have to carry it to fruition."* — *Senior IT Executive A*
Triggers of improvization	
Legislative changes	*"A law was passed that required us to install GPS tracking in all our trucks in October 2008… This is because of the hazardous materials that we were transporting."* — Senior IT Executive A
Managerial alertness	*"Our Senior Executive Vice President used to study in Japan. He reads a lot of Japanese books (on technology). QR-Code was one of the technologies he found… He was very keen on QR-Code. He saw many applications of QR-Code in Japan, so he told us that we must think of an application that uses QR-Code in CCP."* — Head of IT Department

(Continued)

Table 3. *(Continued)*

Enactment of improvization

Overlap of planning and execution	*"We had no idea what to do with QR-Code initially, so we did some study on it. We had to come up with some application. We thought of replacing our current one-dimensional code with QR which is two-dimensional. But we hesitated because there was not much value in doing so... We experimented quite a bit. For example, we tried to print out big pictures of QR-Code and paste them on the side of trucks, hoping the reading process can speed up in that way."* — Head of IT Department
Developing and experimenting with other alternatives	*"Instead of QR-Code, we thought about using RFID ... we also thought of using this wireless platform called ETC, which is used by the government for cashless toll charges. We went as far as developing a number of trials using these technologies. But we quickly realized that they would not work... In the case of RFID, under certain frequencies, it will cause a static shock, which is a definite 'no–no' for us since a lot of our materials are flammable... The case of ETC was infuriating ... we wanted to see their management with our plans but they kept avoiding us because they did not want to deal with a private sector firm."* — IT Manager

Improvizational outcomes

Cost savings from improvization	*"Let's take for example the case of IP-PBX. We could have spent NT\$5 million on a world-renowned brand like Avaya, or we can spend NT\$1 million to piece together our own. Which would you choose? A NT\$5 million solution or NT\$1 million solution? In the end, it is really up to you ... as long as it works, the top management doesn't care how it is done ... but of course, the savings are tangible."* — Senior IT Executive A
Effective support for business operations	*"For example, the time in UK is 8 hours behind Taipei. It does not make sense for a manager in Taipei to wait in the office after working hours for an early call from UK. Our IP phone solved the problem. The manager can be at home or outside. As long as there is internet, he can be reached by his UK counterpart..."* — Deputy Head of IT Department
	"We know our system is used extensively by people in the factories because they would call us immediately whenever they experience any problems. It shows that our system has a huge impact on their daily work. We feel proud that our work has made good contributions to their work." — Senior IT Executive B

Discussion Questions

1. What is the concept of enterprise agility? And what is the existing perspective on IT-enabled enterprise agility?
2. What is organizational improvization? And how does it process?
3. In the second step, why is a trigger necessary for the initiation of improvization in IT deployment? What should the trigger be in order to effect improvization in IT deployment? How can improvization triggers be detected and acted upon?
4. How can improvization be enacted in the third step? What is the feature of improvization in IT deployment of CCP? And how can improvization lead to agility in IT deployment in the last step?

11

360buy.com
(Renamed JD.com in 2013)

Peiying Huang

Introduction

It was a fine Monday morning in November 2011. Shen Hao Yu, the COO of 360buy.com, had just finished regular meeting with top managers of the company. In the meeting, they discussed the "Asia One" project. The project aimed to build seven large-scale automatic warehouses all over China to enhance the capacity of the company's logistics. It would make the company more flexible in adjusting its delivery service based on customer changing needs. The first warehouse that was under construction was located in Shanghai. The entire area of the warehouse was around 2.47 million square feet. It was expected to be completed by the end of 2013. Once completed, it would become the biggest automatic warehouse in Asia. Liu Qiang Dong, the CEO and founder of the company, took the project very seriously. He said: *"Asia One will break through the growth ceilings of the company. If the project fails, the sales volume won't increase any more. If the logistics cannot support the online selling system, various problems will come up, and there will be countless customer complaints.*" He was unsatisfied with the current progress and asked for more aggressive actions in the meeting.

Shen was responsible for the "Asia One" project. He understood the strategic importance of the "Asia One". E-commerce companies usually outsourced delivery service to logistics companies for the purpose of cost-saving and better service. However, logistics companies were providing poor delivery service back to that time. Most e-commerce companies realized this problem but still accepted the poor delivery service for cost-saving purpose. As a result, logistics became the biggest headache for e-commerce companies in China. In order to control the quality of delivery service, 360buy.com made a strategic change from outsourcing logistics to building its own logistics. So the company launched the "Asia One" project. However, Shen also realized the difficulty of building the mega-size automatic warehouses. It mainly came from the pressure of processing a huge amount of sales orders. The volume of individual sales orders had exceeded 1 million per day. This required the new warehouses to handle a huge amount of delivery orders daily, which caused a burden-some task of managing information. Although he understood competent information management was critical for the success of "Asia One," he had less experience in making use of information to improve business performance. He recalled that the IT department had done a good job in facilitating effective information management across the company in the past few years. So he was going to talk with some of the experienced colleagues from IT department to get advice.

Industry Background

The concept of e-commerce was imported into China in the 1990s. However, due to low Internet penetration rate and the subsequent collapse of the Internet bubble, the development of e-commerce had been hindered for several years. The situation was improved after the outbreak of Severe Acute Respiratory Syndrome (SARS) in 2004. To avoid being infected with SARS, people stopped from shopping in bricks-and-mortar stores, which provided a great opportunity for the growth of e-commerce. Several famous e-commerce companies were born in that period, such as Dangdang.com, Joyo.com, Taobao.com, and 360buy.com. In 2004, the growth rate of Chinese e-commerce reached 73.7%. The sales volume of the whole industry reached 350 billion Chinese dollars. Since then, Chinese e-commerce industry has experienced a rapid growing period. During this period, the online shopping environment has been improved with the emergence of third-party online payment platform (such as Alipay), the advancement of product online presentation technology, and the establishment of online product evaluation system. The number of online consumers increased dramatically at the same time. In 2010, the number of online consumers who had made at least one online purchase reached 185 million, accounting for 40.6% of Internet users.

Organizational Background

360buy.com started its B2C business in 2004. Since then, the company has experienced a remarkable increasing rate of over 200% for seven consecutive years (see Figure 1). This record has been hardly seen in the entire Chinese e-commerce industry. In 2011, the company has become one of the top three B2C companies in China with more than 5.07 billion U.S. dollars sales per year and 36.8% market share (excluding B2C platform companies) (see Figures 2 and 3). Nowadays, the company has more than 40 million users and around 6,000 suppliers offering a comprehensive list of high-quality products. Around 300,000 customer orders are processed daily with more than 50 million page views performed.

As a B2C company, the salience of IT for 360buy.com is without a doubt. Liu Qiang Dong is a technical savvy person who had programmed

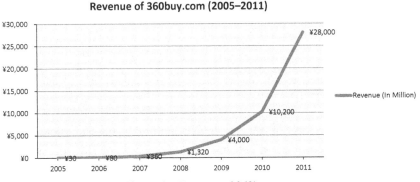

Figure 1. Revenue of 360buy.com.

Source: www.100ec.cn

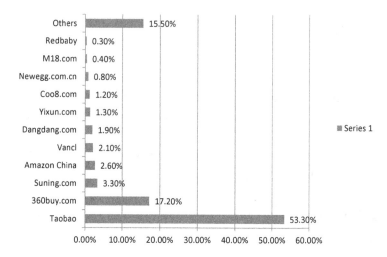

Figure 2. Chinese B2C Sites by Market Share, 2011 (Including Platform Companies).
Source: iResearch Inc.

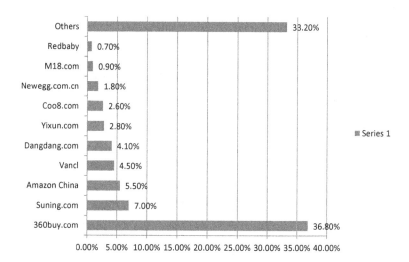

Figure 3. Chinese B2C Sites by Market Share, 2011 (Excluding Platform Companies).
Source: iResearch Inc.

for the websites since its inception. He highlights the significance of excellent user experience in determining the success of B2C companies and strategizes IT as the locomotive of the company toward generating excellent user experience. So the IT department takes the responsibility for driving the innovation and providing more convenient services to meet customer online shopping needs. The sales website of the company is well recognized by consumers as one of the best B2C websites in China. It generates a favorable online shopping environment by facilitating effective communications and interactions with customers, offering customers personalized information, and managing a popular online community for customer interactions.

Compared with the offline business, a prominent feature of e-commerce is that selling a product online has become a highly information-intensive work. This can be interpreted from three aspects. Firstly, the physical layout of a traditional offline shop is replaced by a virtual environment full of all sorts of information. There is a need to organize the information to ensure that customers are able to find the information needed. Secondly, much customer information (e.g., transaction information) can be captured in the online platform. It takes significant efforts to leverage this information for competitive advantage. Thirdly, with the emergence of Web 2.0, user-generated information is highly valued. However, engaging customers in generating valuable information and managing this information remains a headache for most e-commerce companies.

Development of 360buy.com

As the company grows, it incorporates more advanced technologies into sales website for the purpose of attracting and retaining customers. This also brings about different patterns of information management. Based on different types of technologies developed, the development of the company could be divided into three phases: Information-based e-commerce (2004–2009), data-driven e-commerce (2009–2010), and socialized e-commerce (2010–2011).

Information-based e-Commerce **(2004–2009)**

In 2004, the outbreak of SARS precluded people from going shopping in bricks-and-mortar stores, providing an opportunity for the growth of e-commerce. 360buy.com was one of the B2C companies that seized this opportunity. From 2004 to 2009, it centered on reacting to the information needs of online shopping by developing website features that allowed customers to navigate through the web pages readily and gain the relevant information.

Since 2004, the company has witnessed a dramatic growth in online sales. The rapid increase of customer orders brought significant pressures to the website and systems. As a result, the company twice went through website and systems reconstructions in 2007 and 2009. This led to an interactive website and an integrated ERP (Enterprise Resource Planning) system. The ERP system allowed the sales website to retrieve quality information about every aspect of the company, offering strong support to the interactive technical features. It also enabled customer representatives to access various real-time information such as customer information, transaction history and product details. The integrated system brought about high flexibility in reacting to the information needs of online customers. The director of the logistics system development division told Shen,

"The system-reconstruction in 2009 aimed at integrating back-end operational systems. I was the team leader. Before the reconstruction, many systems were isolated. From 2009, we incorporated technologies from external sources. The reconstruction resulted in a set of integrated operational systems."

The director of software quality assurance division described the impact of system integration,

"We have integrated ERP systems in the back-end. Customer representatives can find much relevant information from the systems, such as customer information, transaction information, including some inquiries about the products."

As quality information was available, the company developed an interactive sales website that enabled customers to find relevant information readily. Liu highlighted the significance of excellent user experience in determining the success of B2C companies, and took charge of the overall design of the website. The director of website product division said,

"Actually user experience design is a broad topic that requires the efforts of the whole company. Our boss is the chief decision maker for user experience design. He will make the final decision for user experience design issues."

A project team was designated to solve user experience design (UED) issues. This enhanced the organizational ability in designing the overall layout and individual components to meet the information needs of online shopping. The website offered customers many helpful technical features, such as a search engine, product navigation tools, and online order tracking. It also provided effective communication tools (e.g., online Q&A, e-mail connection with customer representatives, and product review tools) (see Figures 4 and 5) in case customers failed to find relevant information. The director of website data management division explained to Shen,

> "We have a unified and consistent plan for website design that helps solve design issues, such as how the template is embedded in the website, where to place an advertisement, what kinds of recommendation should be provided. … It includes website design, website development, interactivity design, and user research."

While the communication tools allowed customers to gain more relevant information, they also raised a challenge to the company. To ensure

Figure 4. Online Customer Representative of 360buy.com.

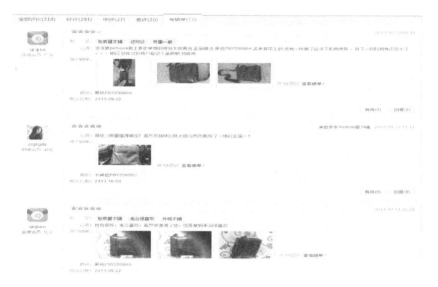

Figure 5. Online Customer Review from 360buy.com.

excellent user experience, the company should be able to provide a timely response to customer enquiries. In this case, customer enquiries or comments were given higher priority as compared to the internal needs of the company. Furthermore, customer representatives were given restricted time to offer a response to customer enquiries. This resulted in a lot of positive comments on the fast reaction of customer representatives (see Figure 6). Moreover, the company provided a "promise" delivery date to customers after purchase. This helped reduce customer enquiries, thereby relieving the pressure on customer representatives. The director of website data management division explained how they did it,

"Some of the customer enquiries are answered by customer representatives. The integrated systems enable them to retrieve information needed rapidly. Some of the enquiries are answered by the system automatically. So we can reply to customer enquires in a fast manner."

In this phase, the company was responsive to the information needs of online customers. Many customers interacted with the company via communication tools, providing numerous valuable comments. This

Figure 6.　Online Q&A of 360buy.com.

became an important reference for website interactivity design. For example, the company did not provide online order tracking at the beginning. However, customer representatives reported that many customers made frequent enquiries about delivery status after they bought expensive products such as a laptop. Inspired by this information, the IT department developed detailed online order tracking tools to meet information need. By reacting to the information needs of online customers, the company developed the ability to leverage customer comments for competitive actions.

Data-driven e-Commerce (2009–2010)

Given the massive amount of information accumulated from the previous phase, 360buy.com attempted to ferret out useful knowledge from the wealth of information for competitive actions. This led the company to adopt data mining technology. As from 2009, the company has invested considerable effort in using data mining technology to extract valuable insights and offer customized contents to meet the information needs of individual customers.

The company established a data warehouse in 2009, which was the first step towards data mining. A data warehouse served as the infrastructure to mine useful knowledge out of the data available. Subsequently, two divisions of the IT department were assigned to collect and manage data from the sales website and the back-end systems (e.g., ERP system, finance system, and logistics system) respectively. Data collected included customer information, transaction data, and operational data, amongst others. The sales website and the existing systems were adjusted accordingly where additional information was needed. Data management divisions established several algorithms and analytical models to transform data into more meaningful pieces of information, such as detailed customer segmentations. This knowledge thus became the source of many innovative competitive actions. The director of website data management division explained what kind of information was collected,

> "Information collected includes the interactions between customers and the sales website, such as the click-stream data. It also includes the transactional information, such as customer orders and relevant information. Furthermore, the interactions between customers and our customer representatives are also recorded and gathered."

The director of back-end data management division described how they processed the data collected,

> "If there is a need to collect information that is not recorded by existing systems, we will suggest a revision to the existing systems. Once the information needed is collected, we will extract and clean data. Then the data are stored in data warehouse where they are classified by different themes, such as customer online behaviors, transactions, and products."

The foremost value of the knowledge extracted from data was to help the company create customized contents based on the needs of individual customers. Accordingly, the company devised many competitive actions to leverage knowledge. For instance, it launched the e-mail direct marketing (EDM) based on the detailed customer segmentations. EDM was a marketing approach that used e-mail to disseminate promotion information to customers. The company tailored promotion information according to customers' habits and preferences identified, thus increasing the success rate of the marketing campaign. The director of website data management division described the EDM as follows:

"The e-mail Direct Marketing is a good example of how we use data. We collected customer data, transaction data and operation data, and then we analyze data and generated customer segmentations. The results will guide the e-mail Direct Marketing. This approach is also used for advertisement and recommendation."

Another example is offering customized recommendations for customers during the shopping process. The recommendation tools increased exposure to products that might meet customer needs, and thereby encouraged impulsive purchase (see Figure 7). Since an improved understanding of customers' habits and preferences was available, the company developed the ability to tailor its offers to meet customer needs. The co-director of website product development division responsible for recommendation systems said,

"We offer customized recommendations to meet the preferences of individual customers. For example, a store might recommend beer when people buy diapers. Why? The buyers could be men. It is possible that they also want to buy beer. The data mining technology allows us to discover this kind of correlations. We can leverage this knowledge to provide customized recommendations."

Despite data mining technology having demonstrated its value in facilitating online sales, the members of the company continued to explore

Figure 7. Customized Recommendation from 360buy.com.

various applications to take full advantage of the technology. IT professionals attempted to understand business needs, and sought to identify the alignment between business and the functions of technology. The company benefited considerably from data mining, leading to the formation of an organizational climate that treasured the value of information. This was reflected in a saying from the company, "let the data speak." The director of website product division explained,

> "It would be very difficult for business people to clarify their requirements. They don't know to whom the website should provide recommendations. However, we (IT professionals) are more capable to do it. We can gain knowledge from analyzing massive amounts of data. So it is important for us to extract knowledge from data to help achieve business goals of the company."

Furthermore, the entrepreneurial culture of the company incited organizational members to aggressively leverage this technology for more competitive actions. The director of software quality assurance division said,

> "360buy.com is a startup company growing with a high speed. We considered ourselves as entrepreneurs. Many middle managers joined the company with a lower salary compared with the previous job and they are strongly motivated to make contributions to the growth of the company."

In this phase, the company took the initiative of identifying the habits and preferences of individual customers and customizing its offers to meet the needs of individual customers. As increasing customers shopping on the company's sales website, a large amount of customer information was captured. This information provided an essential source for analyzing customer behavior and generating a deeper understanding of customer needs. This was done with the support of data mining technology. By taking the initiative to understand customers' habits and preferences, the company developed the ability to leverage valuable customer data for competitive actions.

Socialized e-Commerce (2010–*Present*)

Virtual communities (e.g., Facebook) assume increasing importance as Internet users are spending more time on them. Many firms have launched virtual communities for their customers with the aim to increase sales, gain positive word of mouth, and increase information sharing. 360buy.com also took initiative to leverage this emerging technology for competitive actions. It has invested a lot in establishing a virtual community where its customers can share their shopping experiences, discuss products, and make product recommendations.

In 2008, Liu set up a strategic goal of "socializing" the sales website with a virtual community, which meant that the sales website was going to host a virtual community. He indicated that a virtual community allowed customers to review products, share shopping experiences, and acquire latest product information. In 2010, the company officially launched a virtual community (see Figure 8). A division of the IT department was designated to take responsibility for the development and management of the virtual community. The company hired a lot of talented people who were good at developing social network sites to propel the

Figure 8. Virtual Community of 360buy.com.

development of the online community. Liu expected the virtual community to enhance the stickiness of the sales website by facilitating interactions between the company and customers, as well as among customers. The director of platform architecture division told Shen,

> "Our boss talked about the development of a user community last year. He emphasized the significance of a user community and strategized it as a tool to 'socialize' the e-commerce website."

However, before the virtual community could contribute to the sales website, it was confronted with the challenge of attracting and retaining members. The company designed the policy elements and information cues of the virtual community to foster a sense of belonging. Some of the examples include granting members access to customer representatives to encourage feedback, ranking memberships into different levels (e.g., silver and golden) and showing membership information in members' profiles to signal their contributions. Furthermore, the company established the synergy of the sales website and the community to transform customers into community members. The linkage between the sales website and the community was established by showing the products brought from the sales website in members' profile pages. The co-director of website product development division responsible for transaction systems shared his thought on the development of the virtual community,

> "The most important thing of building a user community is to develop a variety of applications, such as product review, product show-off (an application that allows users to post the pictures of products they bought) and so on. This helps attract users."

The company strove to nurture the behavior of sharing shopping experiences to sustain the virtual community in the long run. It arranged the layout and organized the contents of the virtual community to nurture sharing behavior. For example, members were encouraged to upload images to show off the products bought from the sales website. These posts were displayed in the home page of the community, making their contributions more obvious to other members (see Figure 9). The contents were organized into different circles, attracting members with similar

Figure 9. Products Show-off from 360buy.com.

interests, so that they shared a common topic to discuss. Furthermore, incentives (e.g., bonus points or coupons) were provided to behaviors that contributed to the common wealth of the community. The co-director of the website product development division responsible for recommendation systems gave an example,

> "A successful story is the 'Tui Jian You Li' (which means you can get benefits from recommending products to your friends). Customers can develop their own circles in the user community. We provide technical supports for them to recommend a product to their circles. We also provide some incentives to a successful recommendation."

The director of the website product division described the sharing behaviors of community members,

> "Customers post many product reviews in the user community. This attracts many customers, leading to more purchases and more members willing to share their product experiences. … Currently, the sharing behaviors in online community are driven by incentives, such as bonus points. Consumers share information or attend discussion for the attractive bonus points."

In this phase, the company attempted to establish a virtual community for more useful information and increased sales. The virtual community allowed its customers to share their shopping experiences, discuss products and make product recommendations. Customers may find helpful information from the community to complement the limited information presented in the sales website. The company can discover many innovative ideas from the discussions among community members. By encouraging customers to create value for the virtual community, the company developed the ability to leverage customers' innovative ideas for competitive actions.

The Next Stage

After talking with his colleagues, Shen reconfirmed the critical role of information management in meeting customers' changing needs. This could also be the key to the success of Asia One. The Asia One project will provide a great opportunity for the company to differentiate itself from its competitors. 360buy.com will become the first B2C company that builds up its own logistics. If the project succeeds, it will offer the company with the flexibility in its delivery service. However, if the project fails, it will become a disaster, as the company has invested heavily in the project. Shen understood that the new warehouses must be able to trace products efficiently and dispatch items automatically. This relies heavily on IT systems that can facilitate effective information processing. He believed that the IT department would play a significant role in the development of the automatic warehouses. Next, he needed to talk with Liu about his new thoughts and prepare a proposal for the new IT systems.

Discussion Questions

1. How does the interaction of people, information, and technology affect business performance in 360buy.com?
2. What are the practices that lead to high information orientation in 360buy.com?

3. What are the key challenges in the development of the "Asia One"? If you were Mr. Shen, how would you propose to resolve these challenges?

4. What are some of the lessons learned from the previous success of 360buy.com that can be replicated in the development of the "Asia One"?

12

UFIDA

Mao Mao

Introduction

It was another cloudy and misty day in October 2013 in Beijing. Mr. Wu Hao walked into his boss' office. It was his second year since he was assigned to charge UFIDA's cloud service platform, i.e., Unified Application Platform (UAP). "The UAP has been running very well and an increasing population of firms have joined it. It is a big step for our cloud computing strategy. A few days ago, I read an internal report, which says more and more of our small clients who wish to have a cost-effective IT solution for their business management," the boss said. "Do you mean we should introduce cloud service to those small enterprises?" asked Mr. Wu. "Yes, that is what I am considering. You know Changjet, our subsidiary firm, has been providing IT solutions to small and micro firms for a long time. I think it's time to initiate cloud-based IT solution in Changjet. Are you willing to lead this program in Changjet?" asked the boss. "Sure, of course," answered Mr. Wu. "We can develop our cloud computing products for those small-sized clients, so we can fill this niche market," said the boss. "Right. Those clients usually cannot afford to deploy IT from the top to the bottom, so cloud service is definitely a cost-effective approach for them. It will help them to focus on their core business by cutting the budget on IT infrastructure building," said Mr. Wu. "Yes, you make the point." said the boss. "But does it mean we will gradually retreat from traditional software market, I mean, the packaged software selling during this process?" asked Mr. Wu. "No, not really. I think we can still provide packaged software to our clients in parallel to our cloud service. It means our software services will be accessed in two different channels. The clients can choose one of them in their benefit," the boss clarified and continued "UFIDA is shifting toward its third phase, i.e., cloud computing era. It's an inevitable trend in the IT industry, especially after the 2008 financial crisis. Cost-effective becomes tremendously important for all firms, no matter its size or industry or so, and let our small clients enjoy such benefits as well...." Although Mr. Wu has been working in the UAP division for a long time, he clearly knows that small enterprises have different concerns about IT adoption from large enterprises. Hence, the method of providing cloud service on UAP should be different from cloud service for those small firms. There are many other detailed issues to consider for developing this cloud platform, such as pricing of cloud service, security of data storage, etc.

Industrial Background

The management software industry has developed for over 20 years in China. It can be summarized into three phases. The first phase ranged from 1992 to 1999. In this period, The Treasury Department of China published the "Accounting Computerization Working Standard" whitepaper, which initiated a widespread progress towards accounting computerization in public and private sectors. This policy also provoked many intellectual with some accounting background to develop financial software. Mr. Wang Wen Jing, the founder of UFIDA and Mr. Xu Shao Chun, the founder of Kingdee are two typical figures in this period. Accounting computerization has a significant impact on accounting processing efficiency. The second phase was from 2000 to 2005. In this period, many local software firms started to provide Enterprise Resource Planning (ERP) solutions, which were regarded as an extension from traditional accounting software. In the meanwhile, some other management software, such as SCM, CRM, HRM, and PLM, were provided for the sake of enterprise management. All in all, these IT solutions covered the whole manufacturing process from supplying, stocking, manufacturing, and marketing. The third phase started from 2006. It was a new era for the software industry. The traditional software products were overturned by a new concept of "Cloud Computing." Cloud computing was becoming even more popular after 2008 as a result of increasing awareness of operational cost in many industries. Many organizations were looking for a new cost-effective IT solution for their business management. Cloud computing can provide organizations with cloud-based application software with low IT deployment investment and reasonable charging scheme.

In 2013, the management software industry in China had achieved over 20 billion RMB sales revenue, with 17% annual increase rate on average for the last five years. In 2008, the financial crisis significantly restrained Small and Medium sized Enterprises (SMEs) demand for management software because of limited IT budget. In contrast, high end large enterprises were going to adopt ERP system at enterprise level in order to make their operational process more efficient. In 2012, the Chinese government started to stimulate and support small and micro enterprises development through tax release, financial assistance, and information service. All of these motivate increasing adoption of management software in small and micro enterprises. Hence, SMEs have increasing percentage of management software demand compared to large enterprises in the past three years.

In terms of product market segmentation (see Figure 1), ERP is still the most marketable product, which comprised almost half of management software market. SCM and financial software altogether accounted for 30% of the market. Hence, resources planning, supply chain management, and accounting management are three most concerned areas in a company. In terms of market share of different software vendors in this market (see Figure 2), we can see that UFIDA has the biggest market share of 13%. The next three followers are SAP, Kingdee (another local software vendor), and ORACLE.

In 2013, the trend of the management software industry can be described with a few keywords like cloud computing, mobilization, and socialization. First of all, cloud computing has become a new business model for many

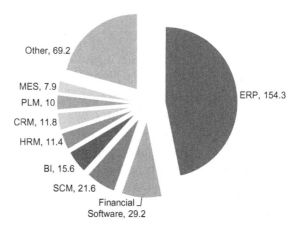

Figure 1. 2013 Management Software.

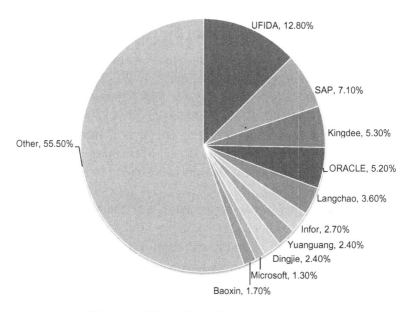

Figure 2. 2013 Software Vendors Market Share.

software vendors. Compared to traditional management software, one obvious advantage of cloud computing is its cost-effectiveness. Since the 2008 financial crisis, cost management became a vital issue for many corporations. However, the adoption and implementation of traditional packaged management software incurs substantial IT infrastructure and platform building cost. On contrast, cloud computing does not require clients to do IT infrastructure construction. Enterprises also pay for IT solution based on their usage, just like paying for electricity and water usage. Many software vendors have provided cloud-based services to their clients. UFIDA established a UAP, on which different applications are developed and provided. Kingdee released K/3 Cloud, which is positioned to SMEs market. SAP and ORACLE also provided their cloud services for their customers. Secondly, with increasing population of mobile phone users, clients have a high demand for doing their business on mobile terminals, such as cell phone, tablet, and laptop. Hence, many software vendors have incorporated mobile business function in their product design. Thirdly, as social network sites have become a part of our online life, enterprises are seeking for close relationship with their clients, suppliers, or business partners through socialized services. Hence, this feature is also embedded in the design of many management software. UFIDA, the biggest player in this market, has to face relentless competition in the future.

UFIDA's Background

In 1988, Mr. Wang Wen Jing worked as a government agent with a decent payment. It was his fifth year serving in the public sector after graduation. At that time, he was in charge of the accounting computerization program. During his work, he found that financial software was needed by almost every organization for accounting management. He realized that financial software is a marketable product in the process of accounting computerization. Then, he made a stunning decision to leave the admirable public sector. Together with Mr. Su Qi Qiang, he initiated a start-up software firm. In a nine-meter square room, with borrowed fifty thousand RMB and a desktop, two youngsters founded the "UFIDA Financial Software Association." They developed software in the evening and sold their product in the daytime. At that time, computer software was still running on disk operating system (DOS). Software was still a novelty to many people and organizations. Software was a stand-alone application on each computer. Mr. Wang recalled that most employees didn't even know how to type Chinese characters in the computer. Technically, this was the first stage of UFIDA, selling stand-alone DOS-based financial software. Fortunately, UFIDA made eighty thousand sales revenues in the first year.

After five years' development, UFIDA became the biggest financial software vendor in terms of its market share in 1993. In 1996, UFIDA stepped into the second stage. First of all, UFIDA became the first local ISO 9001-certified software vendor. It ensured UFIDA to produce large-scale, standardized, high-quality software. Secondly, UFIDA started to cooperate with Microsoft. One year later, UFIDA published the first Windows 95/NT-based financial software, which signalled its shift from DOS-based software to Windows-based software. Windows and UFIDA also promised to promote each other's products in their marketing events. In this period, UFIDA also established thousands of distribution hubs across China in order to serve increasing clients. It was also in this period that UFIDA reinforced its market position with fast market expansion.

Around 1999, UFIDA came to the third stage of its development. The appearance of Internet changed the manner in which business partners and an organization's internal departments cooperated. Marketing, manufacturing, supply chain, accounting, and stocking were closely integrated, thanks to Intranet or Internet. Enterprises needed a comprehensive solution for their business management of different functions. In response to this market change, UFIDA accelerated its strategic shift from a financial software firm to a management software firm. By cooperating with IBM and Lenovo, UFIDA published ERP, HRM, CRM, EAM, SCM, etc. In order to promote ERP adoption in different enterprises, UFIDA launched an "experience marketing" strategy in 2004. UFIDA established over 20 ERP experience hubs in Chinese first-tier cities. Enterprise executives can play different roles (e.g., director manager, marketing manager, administration manager, HR manager, etc.) in an ERP-assisted business situation. So, they had a first-hand experience of the advantages of ERP system. Such marketing strategy significantly promoted UFIDA's ERP products selling. It helped UFIDA become the biggest ERP vendor in China.

On December 23, 2010, UFIDA published the "S+S (i.e., software + service)" strategy, which meant UFIDA would provide IT solutions in both traditional packaged software and cloud service. This two paralleling channelled IT solutions signalled the fourth stage in UFIDA development, i.e., cloud era. It was another strategic shift from a traditional management software vendor to cloud-based service provider. Mr. Wang thought that it is a transitional phase to provide both cloud-based service and traditional packaged software. UFIDA would finally transfer to a cloud dominant service provider. In 2012, UFIDA published UAP, on which application are developed and sold to large enterprises. In 2013, UFIDA planned to provide public cloud service to small and micro firms in the future. Until now, UFIDA has maintained its lead position in the management software market in China for over 9 years. It is also the biggest software vendor in the Asia–Pacific area.

Development of UFIDA

Traditional Software Solution

Customer orientation is the basic principle in UFIDA's development. It is not only reflected by its establishment, but also embodied in its growth. Because of customer orientation, UFIDA can precisely perceive the change of user requirements and notice the shift of market trend on time. Mr. Zhen, the senior deputy head, Marketing Division of UFIDA Group, said:

> "When Mr. Wang, the founder of UFIDA, was still working in the public sector in 1988, he was spearheading the development, promotion and implementation of financial software. He found that financial software was needed by both government agencies and private enterprises. He thought it was a promising business opportunity and decided to establish a software firm in response to accounting computerization. A few years later, UFIDA became the biggest financial software vendor in China. In the early 1990s, when Mr. Wang was visiting clients in Yanhai and Dongguan cities, he observed that many clients started to pay more attention on manufacturing management. Hence, Mr. Wang realized that UFIDA had to shift to a management software vendor."

This strategic transformation was a milestone in UFIDA's history. Initially, due to lack of experience, UFIDA decided to focus on small and medium-sized enterprises. It also avoids direct competition with international software vendors, such as SAP and ORACLE. In 1997, UFIDA launched its first U8 product for medium-sized firms. Many clients were subordinate enterprises of conglomerates. Mrs. Yang, the assistant head, U8 Product Division, said:

> "U8 is a product line for firms which grow from a start-up to a medium-sized company. Unlike small firms, medium-sized companies need a comprehensive corporate management, including finance, manufacturing, supply chain, etc. Therefore, U8 provides them with a comprehensive IT solution suited to their business development and management. We can help our clients have a smooth transition from T series product[1] to U8."

Gradually, UFIDA gained more experience during the implementation of U8 for its clients. At the same time, some of the clients evolved from medium-sized to large companies. They had high requirements for company-level informatization. In order to satisfy these companies' needs, UFIDA released its first North Carolina (NC) product aimed at large companies or conglomerates in 2002. Therefore, since then, UFIDA had covered every market segment from SMEs, to large companies and conglomerates. Mr. Huang, the product manager, NC Product Division, said:

> "In 2000, we dedicated to develop ERP products for large enterprises. Many of our original clients at that time had become group corporate. In 2002, we launched NC 2.0, which was an extension of U8. In between, we had a transitional product called 9X (i.e., NC 1.0). The first version of NC was basically still a financial management system. In the following versions, we incorporated supply chain management, manufacturing management, HR management, etc. All of these contributed to a comprehensive ERP solution. In NC 5.7, we also added capital asset management, fund management, and budget management, which are particularly important for group enterprise."

With the fast development of UFIDA, it became the largest management software vendor in China in 2005. In the meanwhile, clients required higher product performance and more industrial-specific individuality.

---

[1]T series is a product line for small and micro firms. It was developed by Changjet, Co.

It raises a big challenge for UFIDA to satisfy each client's customization. It provoked UFIDA towards the strategy of industrial chain cooperation. Mrs. Yang, the assistant head, U8 Product Division, said:

> "For U8 product line, we have a large number of clients, and it's almost impossible to meet each client's specific requirement about our product. So, our strategy is to outsource industrial-specific features development to our business partners, who definitely know much better about our clients than us."

Such individuality requirements from customers also has an influential impact on the software development process. The traditional rigid and inflexible developing method does not fit to fast changing client's needs. Mrs. Yang, the assistant head, U8 Product Division, said:

> "In the past, we used the traditional software development process, i.e., Waterfall Model". This process can be specified into four phases: planning, defining, design and development, and test. However, when we stepped into the Internet era, this traditional method is not immune to fast changing requirements from our clients. With the traditional method, we can only incorporate clients' requirements into the next version of our product. In order to solve this problem, we adopted a process called "Agile Development Process", which allows multilateral communication among different participants, such as UFIDA, ISVs, clients, and other business partners. We invite clients and partners to join our product development process from the very beginning. We twist the product according to their feedback from time to time."

In order to maintain a competitive advantage, UFIDA has to focus on its core business. So, for implementation service and after-sales services, UFIDA adopts the same strategy of outsourcing. Mr. Wang, the CEO and president of UFIDA, said:

> "Like many international software vendors such as SAP and ORACLE, we decided to outsource 80% of our IT solutions' implementation and after-sales services. It is because nowadays we do not have enough human resources to serve each of our clients. In addition, our business partners can take the advantage of their expertises to serve our clients better. So, we just play our main role as a solution provider; this is an appropriate business strategy for us."

For traditional management software vendors, market diversification and customer individuality are inevitable. UFIDA has changed its business pattern and product development process in order to survive in this competitive environment. Although UFIDA has grounded firmly on this traditional software market, it has to renovate again to adapt to a new era, i.e., cloud computing.

Cloud Computing Solution

Until 2008, NC product line had been developed for 10 years. There had been over 6000 big corporate and conglomerate users. However, there was almost no client from Chinese top group enterprises. Mr. Wang thought it's time to attract more first-tier giant conglomerates to use NFIDA's products. Three years later, UFIDA published NC 6.0, which was a revolutionary product in NC history. NC 6.0 integrates many state-of-the-art functions, such as big data analysis, e-commerce, mobile business, social network, and cloud computing. One particular attraction of NC 6.0 is its low deployment cost. Mr. Liu, the deputy head, UFIDA product division, said:

> "When we first initiated NC 2.0, many clients had only over one or two billion sales revenue. After two or three years, they had achieved over 10 billion sales revenue. After a couple of years, they can grow even bigger. With such speedy expansion, they have to renovate or rebuild their ERP system in order to match the new business pattern and organizational construction. expensive and time-consuming. Therefore, our NC 6.0 is designed to have a flexible dynamic enterprise modelling, which suits enterprises' fast development."

It was more strategically important that the platform (i.e., UAP), which was once exclusively used for NC product development, was open to non-NC developers. UFIDA established a separate division for developing and maintaining this platform. Nowadays, UAP is adopted by UFIDA Group subsidiary firms, such as UFGov, UFAuto, UFMed, and UFFin for their application development. Externally, this platform has been adopted by many Independent Software Vendors (ISVs) in mainland China, Hongkong, Waiwan, Singapore, etc. This indicates UFIDA's move towards the cloud computing market. On 23 December, 2010, UFIDA released its "S+S" business model, i.e., Software + Service. Mr. Wang, the CEO and president of UFIDA, said:

> "S+S business model is based on our judgement about clients' needs for cloud computing service. Our current strategy is "Platform Development, Industrial Chain Cooperation." "S+S" is a transitional phase, in which we still preserve our traditional software products. Ultimately, we will enter a cloud-dominated business pattern."

Cloud computing accelerates the process of vertical specialization. With the cloud computing business model, UFIDA acts as an application developing platform supporter, who provides ISVs a user-friendly developing environment. Mr. Huang, the product manager, NC Product Division, said:

> "In the past, we developed specific IT solutions, i.e., software, for our clients in different industries. Clients usually have their specific requirements about the products. It is a big challenge for us to meet over eight thousand clients' needs across different industries. Nowadays, we only embed key, fundamental features into our platform, and leave detailed design and development to our business partners. Draw an analogy, our product is like a trunk, and our partners add in twigs and leaves. Because those partners know more about customers' needs, they can definitely serve clients better than us."

As UFIDA moves towards cloud computing service, it can focus on its core business (i.e., establishing a stable, safe, and user-friendly platform). At the same time, UFIDA's business partners can get a share in the value chain of application development. It is a win–win situation. The UAP division provides periodic training to internal and external application developers. For those developers, there exists a standard criterion to follow. It ensures the quality and versatility of applications. In order to understand clients' satisfaction, UFIDA also collects feedback from application end users from time to time. In addition, there is a developers' forum for information sharing about designing, operating, supporting, and monitoring issues of the platform.

As more and more large companies transfer to buy applications on the cloud, Mr. Wang considers developing cloud service for small and micro firms. Changjet, a subsidiary firm of UFIDA established in 2008, has been providing IT solutions for over 1.5 clients. Its T+ product line provides different IT solutions for small and micro firms. There have been increasing demands from these clients for convenient tools to solve their business problems. Mr. Ji, the deputy head, Changjet Operation Department, said:

> "In order to meet our clients' needs, we decide to provide cloud service on a platform called CSP. There will be two main parts on this platform. One is application software, which could be traditional packaged software or cloud service. The other part is a forum, which is used by ISVs, clients, and our distributors. We plan to release version 1.0 of this platform by the end of this year."

When UFIDA releases CSP, it will have two cloud computing service lines. UAP is designed for large corporations, and CSP is aiming for small and micro firms. In addition, these two platforms differ from each other in terms of their method of providing cloud service. Mr. Ji, the deputy head, Changjet Operation Department, said:

> "… For large corporations or conglomerates, data security is the most concerned issue in using applications on the cloud. So, the UAP-based cloud service is provided (brought) exclusively to (by) our clients as their private cloud. In contrast, small and micro firms are concerned more about cost and convenience of our applications, so public cloud is more cost-effective and appropriate for them."

Despite such difference between cloud services on UAP and CSP, both of them help saving clients IT budget compared to traditional packaged application software. When using IT solution on the cloud, clients do not need to deploy IT infrastructure internally. It saves clients' expenditure on maintaining or upgrading their system. In addition, the cloud computing business model also changes the cycle of software development, especially shortens the developing cycle. Mr. Ji, the deputy head, Changjet Operation Department, said:

> "In the past, the software development cycle duration was normally one year or half a year. Before the software designing and developing phase,

there is a period for collecting clients' needs conducted by a professional team. When developing application on the cloud, clients' needs or requirements are continuously collected in the whole process of application development. Developers should revise their application whenever new requirements come in. In addition, our developing team becomes smaller, with around 10 to 20 people for each application development. Then, different applications are integrated into a comprehensive IT solution. So, the development cycle is shortened to one quarter or even one month."

As a platform operator, Changjet attempts to provide ISVs a safe, stable, and user-friendly developing platform. ISVs play an important role in connecting us to our clients. Unlike large corporates, small firms usually do not need a consultation about a comprehensive IT solution. They are concerned more about what kind of tools can practically solve their business problems. They have a very specific purpose of using a particular application. Mr. Ji, the deputy head, Changjet Operation Department, said:

> "CSP is established to provide cloud services to small and micro firms. If clients decide to come to this platform, they will find appropriate tools (i.e., applications) to meet their requirements. If ISVs decide to come to our platform, they will find verified and useful developing tools and services assisting them to develop applications at low cost. We would also help those ISVs to promote their applications to accurate clients. Although now we are still serving our clients by selling packaged software, in the long run we will transfer to cloud-based services to those small and micro clients."

Concluding Remarks

The business concept of UFIDA is "Continuous Innovation, Balanced Development". The CEO of UFIDA, Mr. Wang, said compared to continuous innovation, balanced development is more important. According to buckets effect, how much of a bucket filled with water, does not depend on the highest piece of wood on the sides of casks, but rather depends on the shortest piece on the sides of casks. Mr. Wang believes a balanced development of UFIDA ensures the capability of continuous innovation. UFIDA also thinks highly of human resources management. For UFIDA, human capital is the most important capital in the company. UFIDA places great emphasis on talent pool building. Staffs are recruited and promoted on the basis of intellectual ability and their contributions. In order to improve staffs' organizational commitment, UFIDA have launched two equity incentive plans. The plans cover 20% of company's staffs, compared to average 5% of most local software firms. Hence, these equity incentive plans benefit not only firm's senior manager and executives, but also cadre employees and some experts. UFIDA involves its succession plan, which selects those with comprehensive management skills to lead UFIDA in the future.

UFIDA also has an industry–university–institute cooperation basis. In U.S.A., UFIDA established a silicon R&D institution, which invites many industrial experts for platform design and construction research and other research works. UFIDA has a close relationship with many Chinese universities, such as Tsinghua University, Chinese Academy of Science, Beijing University of Posts and Telecommunications, etc. Those universities have strong research ability in computer science. UFIDA can benefit from their research outcome. By integrating different resources, UFIDA reinforces its technological strength to solve practical problems.

UFIDA clearly knows that cloud computing has an unprecedented impact on software industry. Thanks to the customer orientation principle throughout UFIDA's development, it timely adjusts its strategy to adapt itself to this new era. In this process, UFIDA not only changed the manner in which business partners cooperated, but also altered its application development process to make it more agile. However, there are still many issues in this pivotal transitional period for UFIDA to solve. For example, business data safety and privacy is always concerning cloud computing adopters. None of the firms want the data of their customers leaked out to competitors. None of the firm's senior executives want external personnel read the firm's internal report before they read it. Hence, in order to attract more companies to buy cloud service, UFIDA has to establish a safe and stable platform. In addition, providing cloud-based service along with traditional package software may jeopardize the selling of packaged software. Such strategic transition needs to be safe, stable, and smooth.

References

http://finance.sina.com.cn/leadership/crz/20051115/14132120491.shtml.
http://www.forbeschina.com/review/201110/0012516.shtml.
http://wiki.mbalib.com/wiki/%E7%94%A8%E5%8F%8B%E8%BD%AF%E4%
    BB%B6%E5%85%AC%E5%8F%B8.
http://baike.baidu.com/view/118599.htm?fromTaglist.
http://doc.mbalib.com/view/c4e76ae2b258ccc6c036976e988201d6.html.

Discussion Questions

1. As a two-channeled IT solution provider, UFIDA provides two different IT solution approaches. One is traditional packaged software, and the other is cloud computing services. Describe the differences between these two approaches?
2. Use SWOT methodology to analyze the strength, weakness, opportunities, and threats of the cloud computing service.
3. As described in the teaching case material, UFIDA in 2012 published UAP as a service to ISVs, who can develop and provide applications on it. One year later, UFIDA decided to launch another platform called CSP, which is also an application development support platform. What is the difference between these two platforms?

13

Tencent

Derek Wenyu Du

Company Background

China has the world's largest internet population at 513 million, which is 34% of its total population and which grows at an annual rate of 12% (CINIC, 2012). This population creates a vibrant market that attracts both local and international players. In most sectors, local players outperform their international counterparts. For example, Baidu controls 70% of searches in China, twice as much as Google and Bing combined, and TaoBao has assumed eBay's position as the dominant e-commerce platform and forced the latter to withdraw from China. Although local players have been criticized for imitating their Western counterparts, many are very innovative. For example, the virtual products and various business models around these products are first introduced and popularized by Chinese companies that are led by Tencent (see Figure 1 for its market performance on virtual products), and ever since 2008, Tencent has been ranked by Forbes as one of the world's most innovative companies every year. In fact, overemphasis on imitation and overlook on the laudable practice of local players are an important reason that

171

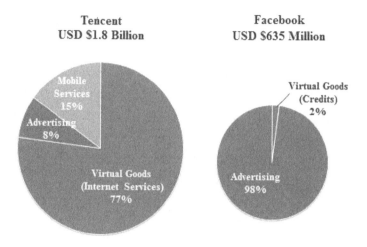

Figure 1.   Revenue Breakdowns of Tencent and Facebook (2009).

deep-pocketed Western veterans are defeated by young, poorly funded local companies.

Tencent is a typical example of a local company, in which many good local practices have been introduced and retained, such as the commitment to stage a perfect user experience and the devotion to cultivate an enthusiastic user community. The company was founded in 1998 by five graduate students from a local university in Shenzhen. Its first product was QQ IM, a local emulation of ICQ. As the first IM product, ICQ was released in 1996 by the Israeli company Mirabilis and subsequently spawned many local versions around the world. Despite much resemblance with its predecessor, QQ had many unique functions that are very popular among Chinese users, such as the auto-lock function that addresses the security concerns of using public computers and a 1-MB installation package that addresses the severe bandwidth constraints faced by most Chinese households. It is indeed these local innovations that differentiate QQ from ICQ and other ICQ variants, and enables QQ to thrive while others including ICQ have ceased to exist.

The success of IM gives Tencent a large user base, which the company leverages extensively to enter other sectors. Today, the company has a broad product portfolio that covers nearly every corner of the internet. This portfolio is divided and managed by four product suites (see Figure 2). The internet service suite covers IM, internet value-added services, and e-commerce business. As the oldest product suite, this line of business was previously the largest revenue center until the rapidly growing entertainment suite took over. The entertainment suite focuses on game development and currently has a wide range of games, from casual to mini-MMO and hardcore MMO. These two suites generate revenue mostly by selling virtual goods, which are also Tencent's largest revenue source. In contrast, advertising contributes only 10% of the revenue and this portion primarily comes from the web and advertising suite, which consists of the web portal and search engine. The mobile service suite consists of multimedia messaging, mobile value-added services, and m-commerce business, and is growing rapidly because of the increasing trend of internet access via mobile devices.

Three strategic divisions coordinate and support these four product suites. The business policy division, as in many other companies, consists of senior managers, but unlike others, it devotes little attention to long-range planning. The COO once commented, "Long-range plans are not helpful as they're most likely irrelevant to reality. But, what's worse is that they pre-set developers' minds and prompt them to see what they want to see rather than reality." Instead, individual product teams are given the discretion to make their own decisions under the coordination of the policy division, which ensures that decisions from the individual teams are in line with the company's overall strategic direction (e.g., the most recent one being "go mobile"), and collaboration among product teams achieve higher strategic value that cannot be delivered by any of them independently. Tencent also maintains two cutting-edge research divisions dedicated to user experience and technical research. The two divisions are positioned at the strategic level, because first, the company's success, as in many local players, is owed to its in-depth user understanding and second, the proprietary technical advancements can curtail rampant imitation across the company's broad portfolio. These two divisions are committed to long-term research, which complements the product teams' near-term focus and prevents product teams from becoming myopic of future user and technical trends.

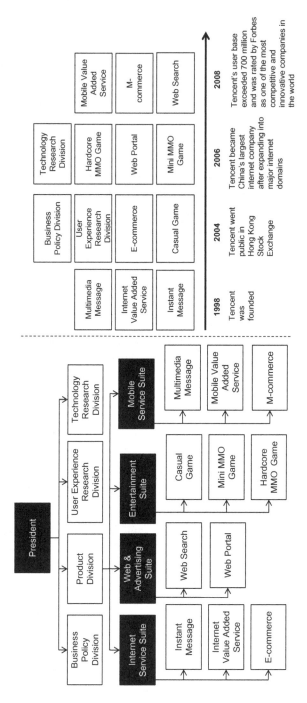

Figure 2. Tencent's Organizational Structure.

Product Development Routine

After a decade of experiments and refinements, Tencent has developed a Sustainable Product Development (SPD) routine that consists of four phases (Tables 1–4). For each phase, we focus on two questions: (1) What is the critical task? (2) How to deliver that task? SPD begins with observation, in which product teams scan the market for new trends and use them to draw new product concepts. The scanning scope is broad, including technologies, user communities and, more importantly, competitors, whose activities are both the best reference for new products and the greatest threats to existing products (Figures 3 and 4). In Tencent, environment scanning is the task of all employees rather than a task assigned to select individuals. During observation at lunch time, we found that the new market trends and recent competitor movements are the two universal discussion topics across lunch tables. Past experience is regularly invoked and blended with the observation, as explained by a senior game developer: "History is like a mirror that helps make better sense of the current situation, and when a new opportunity emerges, we first look back and see if there are similar cases in the past."

Design begins when a new product concept is approved by the business policy division and a product council. Each product suite has a designated product council, and the council is formed by seasoned product managers in the field who access the new product concepts based on their experiences. Innovation is the centerpiece of design. However, rather than expecting innovation to be completely original or cutting-edge, Tencent considers any user experience enhancement to be innovation. One senior developer explained, "Strictly put, there are no innovative or so-called original products in our business. If we have to call some products innovative, they are the ones that are close to user needs." Product managers gather user insights by following a 10/100/1000 rule, which dictates that every month she must survey at least 10 users, read at least 100 user blogs, and collect at least 1000 user logs. The CEO leads by example: "I spend more than 50% of my time with users. For me, that is more important than appearing on TV or attending PR events." The heart of user co-innovation exercise is high-level user commitment. Tencent's success in gaining this kind of commitment owes to its acclaimed "fanatically close relationships

Table 1.   The Critical Task and Its Delivery @ Observation Phase

Scanning the environment to explore new product concepts	*"Internet market is filled with many opportunities and threats. The competition is not about market share or company size. It is about who can **catch the next big thing**. We should never feel complacent. Essentially, we are just one opportunity or threat away from being obsolete."*
	— CEO (*Source*: Archive)
	*"Throughout the years, the market has taught us to be very sensitive to changes. Because technologies, customers, and competitors change every day and often in unexpected manners, we must be **open to all changes and make no assumptions**... But, instead of rushing into new opportunities, we always probe and evaluate them carefully first."*
	— Director, Entertainment Suite (*Source*: Interview)
Leveraging the participation of every employee	*"The (the number of new) trends and the amount of new information in our line of business are amazing. It is not possible to have one central agency for this. Hence, we expect **everyone to act as a keen market observer**... Now in any corner of the company, you may hear discussions about the market, the technologies, and the competitors and good insights usually come from those informal discussions."*
	— Line Manager, Entertainment Suite (*Source*: Interview)
	*"You must **be a member of the target market** in order to understand what is really going on there... All employees (in my division) are active users of popular IMs in the market. For example, I'm using four different ones at the same time. It is important to watch your product closely but **your competitors' products closer** as they are, are often the triggers of new products."*
	— Director, Internet Service Suite (*Source*: Interview)

Table 2. The Critical Task and Its Delivery @ Design Phase

Seeking user insights for new product features	*"We never speculate about what users want. That is a recipe for failure. Instead, **we always actively seek user opinions** and do this as early as possible. Gone are the days when you can lock your staff in a basement, force them to sign a non-disclosure agreement, and develop something that astonishes the world."* — Senior Producer, Entertainment Suite (*Source*: Archive) *"The size of the IM package was controlled at less than 1 MB after users complained about their bandwidth; auto-lock was introduced after learning that many users used public computers in the internet cafe ... These changes are small but have big impacts as they **reach users' deep desires**."* — Product Manager, Internet Service Suite (*Source*: Interview)
Leveraging close relationships with users	*"We **spare no effort in addressing user requests**. We never address user requests perfunctorily, like many of our competitors do. **Users appreciate this,** and they in turn participate in our product design — especially after learning that their suggestions influence millions of people."* — Vice President, Human Resources (*Source*: Interview) *"**Tencent is part of our lives**. Whenever I need to install something, I first go and look for Tencent. The beauty of Tencent products is that you don't worry about technical or usability issues because **they take care of everything** ... the products tend to become the best in the market after a while."* — Undergraduate student, a Tencent fan (*Source*: User Interview)

Table 3. The Critical Task and Its Delivery @ Execution Phase

Responding to user requests in real time	*"We frequently adjust our development schedule because if users don't see their feedback being incorporated quickly, they stop participating. To make the adjustment easier, tasks are divided into small pieces — like the old saying, a small boat is easy to turn."*
	— Senior Engineer, Entertainment Suite (*Source*: Interview)
	*"There was a time I switched from QQ (IM) to MSN. But now, I have switched back because QQ is **getting better every day**. On the contrary, MSN is stagnant. I complained several times about their spamming issue, but nothing was done."*
	— Graduate student, An active Tencent user (*Source*: Customer Interview)
Leveraging coexistence of *ad hoc* and regular teams	*"We've been educated to work with a mentality of change and adapt to the fact that if an urgent task emerges, we need to **put down the task at hand and join an ad-hoc team**... Skill-wise, we don't have much problem, as we have experience working in different teams."*
	— Senior Engineer, Internet Service Suite (*Source*: Interview)
	*"**Employees should be versatile** and comfortable with changes, as they are expected to work in different areas. We adhere to these two principles in our (HR) practice. And when forming ad-hoc teams, we look for **people who complement each other** and recommend them to the product managers who need help."*
	— HR Manager, Gatekeeper's subordinate (*Source*: Interview)

with users". This relationship is built on a set of integrated products that reach users in every aspect of their lives and is built by a team of product managers who devote scrupulous attention to any user request. As an associate product manager proudly announced, "We take total ownership of users' requests, even when they are not about our products … sometimes, we may know more about our competitors' products than they do."

Table 4.　The Critical Task and Its Delivery @ Reflection Phase

Reviewing the past in light of existing problems and trends	*"Sharing at work makes it possible to **combine experience with trends** at that moment. This practice somehow **brings the history to life**. Besides, we really don't have time for reflection that merely summarizes the past but has no foreseeable implications."*
	— Product Manager, Internet Service Suite (*Source*: Interview)
	*"Principles underlying good innovations and products do not change much, and we have seen history repeating itself again and again. But studying history alone is not enough. We need **an updated view of historical lessons**. Otherwise, we will fail again at the same spot, but only in a new context."*
	— Vice President, Mobile Service Suite (*Source*: Archive)
Leveraging the diverse team of natives and new members	*"The most valuable experience and knowledge gained from development are within the employees. Thus, we regularly rotate them so that they can share with more people... The **mix of newcomers and natives** in a team broaden their (natives') perspective and enable them to **escape the mental groove**."*
	— Senior Producer, Entertainment Suite (*Source*: Archive)
	*"We welcome job rotation and working in a new environment. Staying with one product for too long is somewhat boring and not good for career development, as your **thinking becomes narrowed** and you become **less receptive to new changes**."*
	— Senior Engineer, Entertainment Suite (*Source*: Interview)

Execution and design occur in tandem. A senior product manager explained the rationale: "Design and execution are difficult to separate. While it's difficult to develop something without a design, it's equally difficult to design without something concrete for users to feel, touch, and give feedback." This simultaneous act places engineers in a challenging position in which execution must respond to user requests in real-time because late responses upset users and hamper the user-centric design.

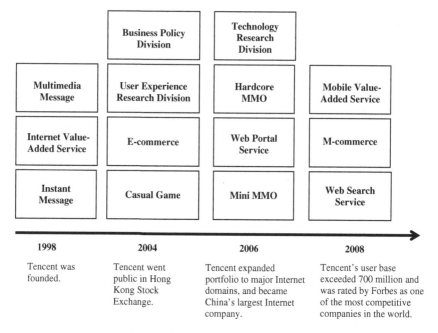

Figure 3.   Tencent's Organizational History.

This challenge is further exacerbated by the unexpected nature of user requests. As a result of these urgent yet unexpected requests, workloads tend to fluctuate, and during the initial launch of a product, the workload often exceeds the focal product team's capacity. To cope with this overwhelming workload, Tencent resorts to *ad-hoc* teams that consist of both the focal team members and temporary recruitment from other teams. A senior developer illustrated the efficacy of these *ad hoc* teams by relating the following story: "Last year, our biggest success was Weechat, which was inspired by competitors doing something similar but at a very basic level... In just two weeks, our product went through 23 updated versions and soon became the market leader. This speed was impossible for many competitors, and we made it possible by recruiting talent across different teams and concentrating them on this single task for a focused period of time." Because special arrangements like this happen frequently, there are many *ad-hoc* teams coexisting with regular teams at any given time. Industry analysts liken this phenomenon to the "coexistence of ambulance and bus lanes."

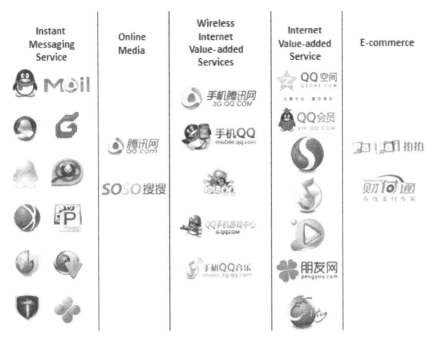

Figure 4. An Overview of Tencent's Products and Services (Year 2013, Interactive Entertainment Service Excluded).

The simultaneous design and execution continue until a product reaches its maturity, when most of the targeted users are acquired and satisfied. There are cases in which products are not well received by users despite the continuous investment, as the CEO explained: "New products have risks, and some will fail. When a product has to fail, we just make sure it fails smart — as we learn something from it." Consistent with the CEO's message, product teams take past experiences, being successful or otherwise, very seriously. Some experiences are summarized into business cases and disseminated through a knowledge management system (KMS) and more are shared by individuals at work. This sharing at work links past experiences with problems at hand and transforms experiences into recommendations that are relevant to the existing problems. Sharing at work is most effective when the product teams consist of members from different backgrounds. Otherwise, if the team members have worked together for a long time, they tend to employ similar thinking patterns that may lock reflection into historical anecdotes. To this end, Tencent develops a regular employee rotation program that intends to create teams that have both native members and new members from other products. Employees also welcome this rotation, as it exposes them to a broader task scope.

Reference

CINIC "China's internet and new media market outlook," China Internet Network Information Center.

Discussion Questions

1. What does the existing literature say about organizations' software product development strategies?
2. What are the challenges faced by Tencent in conducting a new software product development?
3. What are the crucial activities in Tencent's improvization and coordination efforts to overcome the challenges identified in Question 2?
4. What are the key advantages and potential drawbacks of performing improvization in an organization and how are these taken care of in the case of Tencent?

14

Wanhua Chemical Group

Elaine Jing Chen

Industrial Background

Methylene di-p-phenylene isocyanate, most often abbreviated as MDI, is the major ingredient of polyurethane. Polyurethane is a unique material that offers the elasticity of rubber combined with the durability and toughness of plastic. Accordingly, polyurethane is widely used in many industries, including chemical, light, textile, construction, domestic appliance, building materials, transportation, vehicles and aviation, etc. (Figure 1). Therefore, MDI is a chemical product with huge demand.

The global consumption of MDI exceeds 5 million tons per year in 2011. This market is still expanding. Despite the popularity of MDI, the MDI market is very concentrated in a few companies worldwide, because of the technologies and capital cost barriers.

Company Background

Wanhua Chemical Group Co., Ltd. (hereafter "Wanhua") is a listed shareholding chemical enterprise headquartered in Yantai, Shandong, PRC. Founded in 1998, the company has been expanding rapidly in recent

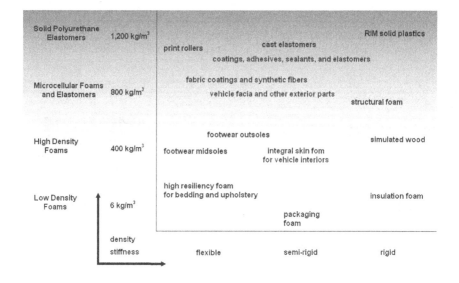

Figure 1.   Different Types of Applications of Polyurethane Materials.

Source: Wikipedia, The free encyclopedia.

years, and has developed world-leading technologies and capacity in the production of MDI. Wanhua now is the largest MDI manufacturer in the Asia–Pacific area and the third largest MDI manufacturer in the world, producing about one-fourth of the global MDI production (see Figure 2). In 2012, Wanhua achieved an annual revenue of US\$2.626 billion and net profit of US\$386.858 million, with over 20,000 employees and 15 branches in 8 countries (see Figure 3).

Despite Wanhua's great superiority in MDI production technologies, which made the company's annual MDI production capability to skyrocket from 15,000 tons in 1999 to 1.2 million tons in 2013, the company had been facing enormous managerial challenges due to existing interconnected routines. On one hand, existing interconnected routines were usually isolated with each other with merely basic coordination, causing the actual business operation of any single customer highly complicated and inefficient. On the other hand, the lack of coordination among interconnected routines eventually inhibited the organization from creatively upgrading its routines by redesigning existing routines

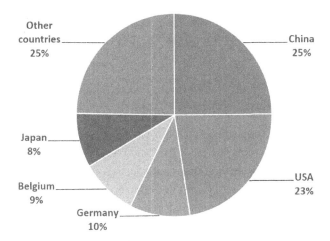

Figure 2. Global MDI Production Share by Region in 2012.

Source: Merchant Research & Consulting Ltd., 2014.

Figure 3. Locations of Wanhua's Global Branches.

with reassembled division of work. Therefore, the organization needed a large-scale reconfiguration of interconnected routines to derive its potential competencies.

Routine Reconfiguration in Wanhua

In order to achieve such a task, the company started from investing heavily on its Enterprise Systems (ES) as a first and basic step to make the integration and optimization of organizational routines technically possible. The implementation of an ERP system in 2008 represents a milestone of such effort. However, ES alone is not sufficient to trigger routine reconfiguration. Hence, triggering and achieving reconfiguration of interconnected routines based on its ES became the crux of Wanhua's transformation.

Routine Reconfiguration Brought by Internal Rotation

Wanhua has a distinctive corporate policy for key managerial talents: All young managers (approximately below the age of 40) shall rotate to the managerial positions in other business functions on a regular basis. This is primarily due to the top management's belief that the most competitive managers shall have comprehensive knowledge about all kinds of business operations. Accordingly, many young managers, who have not reached the top management level, experience drastic job rotations several times. For instance, Mr. Chen, who used to be a manager in the IT Department, later became a manager in the Production Department; Mr. Feng, who used to work in the Production Department, later moved to the Marketing Department as a manager on logistic support; Mr. Chi, who was also a manager in the IT Department, later moved to the Operation Center; and Mr. Kou, who rotated from the IT Department to the Finance Department.

Mr. Shao is one of these young managers, and his experience is very representative regarding the effect of such internal rotation. Mr. Shao had been working for the Finance Department in Wanhua for about 5 years. Despite being a very capable financial expert and knowing little about procurement, he was appointed as an Assistant to General Manager of Procurement Department in early 2013, due to such corporate policy.

Procurement is at the center of Wanhua's business operation. As a large manufacturing company, Wanhua had to purchase over 100,000 types of material every year, with an annual purchasing value of over US$1.7 billion. As the company keeps expanding rapidly, the procurement value was expected to reach US$5.1 billion in 2015. In such circumstances, any single cent saved on the price of a particular material will become huge amount of extra profit. Hence, how to make every purchase utmost economical is very critical to the company. One of the key procurement routines to achieve this is the *supplier selection* routine, since the purchasing price of material directly influences the cost of production.

Before Mr. Shao's arrival, a supplier selection routine was designed and performed as follows: Staff from various business units initiate the purchase request by filling a form indicating the names and quantities of the material needed. The procurement staff then summarize all the material purchasing requests so that they can purchase these material one by one. For each material, the procurement staff will first establish a list of potential suppliers. Then the procurement staff will investigate each candidate to fill a form of price enquires. With the forms of price enquires from all the candidates, the procurement staff will choose the supplier who offers the cheapest price.

When Mr. Shao just joined the procurement department, all the procurement routines were new to him. So he needed to learn how the procurement department carries out its duty from the basics. On one hand, he counted on the ERP system to grasp the most standard operations in the Procurement Department. On the other hand, he participated in the actual operations to strengthen the learning. After extensive efforts for months, he gradually mastered these practices.

As Mr. Shao accumulated expertise in procurement, he noticed that all the existing procurement routines were pursuing the same goal: To maximize the book value of the company, in other words, purchasing the cheapest material for the company according to the marked price. However, such orientation brought about a series of activities in the existing routine, with which he was not satisfied. Just as he asserted: "From the perspective of the existing procurement staff, they depend on market price to finish procurement, in particular, how much does this product take in the market? How much do others pay for the same product? ... They make decisions according to these benchmarks.... So the procurement staff simply gives me a list of quotes, such as "Supplier A sells the product for RMB3000 per unit, Supplier B sells the product for RMB 2000 per unit." However, I think such a form of price enquires is not informative at all.... [Even the chosen supplier offers the cheapest price,] you do not know whether that is really the best one."

Mr. Shao's finance training and practices over years strongly suggests that the procurement activities shall be oriented towards maximized financial value, instead of the maximized book value in the current practice. Knowing the financial value of any product means to have a clear understanding about the cost-structure of this product, as Mr. Shao explained: "... as a financial staff to evaluate the value of certain material, I need to know how many resources does it take to produce this product, how much do these resources cost, what are the profit rate of the suppliers...." By evaluating the financial value of any material purchased, the procurement staffs can minimize the cost of any purchase to the lowest but still reasonable price. Moreover, such a financial-value-driven orientation may benefit Wanhua by engaging long-term strategic supplier partners with cost advantage. Just as Mr. Shao introduced, "By evaluating the financial value of their products, we can find out a supplier providing best quality and lowest cost. Then we can have a long-term collaboration with this supplier." Hence, only when the procurement routines targets at acquiring the highest financial value, can these routines really add most value to the company.

Once he realized this issue, Mr. Shao initiated a revolutionary change on the procurement routines: Instead of aiming at the maximized book value, all the procurement routines shall be financial-value-oriented. Accordingly, a series or arrangement of procurement routines was changed, just as he introduced, "I want the suppliers to report their cost-structure. For instance, how much steel did you use to produce this machine? How many procedures did it take to produce this machine? etc. So I redesigned the form of price enquires, requiring our staffs to figure out more details about our suppliers' quote: The cost of first business process, the cost of second business process ... until we get the complete cost-structure. Eventually, with the cost-structure, and an expected profit rate from the supplier side, we get a final quote. This is how we do it now." In accordance to enriched information required during the procurement routine, the finance department simplified related finance routines as well, since part of the information required for the examination and approval of the procurement decisions has been already provided by the procurement staff.

Routine Reconfiguration Brought by Internal Collaboration

Wanhua's belief in generalist rather than specialist can be found not only in its distinct internal job rotation policy, but also in its in-depth internal collaboration. Wanhua has a well-established tradition that, when collaborating with other departments, staff from one department is encouraged to understand the counter departments as if he or she is a staff in the counter departments. In many cases, such staff can be even interchangeable between both departments. Mr. Kou's experience as follows serves a typical example.

When Mr. Kou just joined Wanhua's IT department as a fresh graduate majored in Computer Science at the end of 2008, his first job was to maintain and adjust the financial IT system for the Finance Department, and to help the financial staff get used to the system. Unlike the conventional IT staff who sit in the computer center most of the time and communicate with system users via phone call, email, and occasional meetings, Mr. Kou's office is located not at the IT Department, but the Finance Department directly. Just as he recalled: "I worked so closely with the financial staff. After our ERP system was implemented in 2008, I had been staying in the Finance Department all day long for about one year. I sat in the office of the Finance Department every day, together with the financial staff." The financial staff actually benefited a lot from such an arrangement, since they had support during the adaptation of the financial IT systems. Just as Mr. Kou said: "We (IT staff) sat with financial staff in the same office every day, and communicate and support them whenever necessary, in order to improve the systems."

Mr. Kou did not simply sit nearby as an isolated technical support for system implementation who only showed up when necessary. Rather, he behaved as if he was an apprentice in the Finance Department while the

Finance Department was completely open to him: He observed all kinds of business operations within the Finance Department, and gradually learnt the financial knowledge behind these operations by both self-learning and consulting financial staff. Moreover, he had not one teacher, but all the financial staff as his teachers, just as he recalled: "During this process I learnt a lot ... I had literally communicated with all the staffs in the Finance Department." Mr. Kou learnt financial knowledge so profoundly that, with more follow-up learning efforts, he was designated to the Finance Department as a manager several years later.

With such close collaboration, Mr. Kou became more capable in managing the IT system and serving system users. On one hand, he is more acute in understanding and sensing system improvement opportunities lying in the junction of finance and IT, as he recalled: "... In the past it might take me two to three days to understand what a user's need was exactly.... Now, with some financial knowledge, I know exactly what the user wants to say, or I can even understand my users' need before they raise the issue out. This is a significant improvement on the efficiency and effectiveness of our job." On the other hand, he became capable of contributing significantly in the integration of business operations via thoughtful IT system design, as he testified: "In the past I only noticed ... very fragmental user needs, and I knew that I need to develop a system [incorporating all those needs without further idea]. But now, we can be very clear about what kind of financial tasks this system is aiming to solve, what are the particular needs, how to plan the financial IT system for the whole company, and how to design the system in order to satisfy those needs." Hence, within one year's time, Mr. Kou could innovatively improve the financial routines by better planning and delivering related IT systems.

One example that Mr. Kou helped improve the financial routines is about the financial routines on the *bank accepted bill*, a kind of negotiable instruments that guarantees payment from the bank in the future.

Before Mr. Kou's initiatives, the management of bank-accepted bill in the Finance Department was designed isolated within subsidiaries. For instance, Subsidiary A had a machine account with its own bank-accepted bills recorded, while the Subsidiary B also had its own machine account for the same purpose. Each subsidiary only took care of its own machine account. As a result, the routine of bank-accepted bill transfer among subsidiaries was quite labor-demanding, since every bank-accepted bill had to be repeatedly entered into machine accounts of different subsidiaries whenever this bank-accepted bill was transferred into a subsidiary.

With his financial knowledge accumulated during close collaboration, Mr. Kou initiated a module in the Systems of Negotiable Instruments at subsidiaries level to synchronize all the records of the bank-accepted bill across different subsidiaries. By doing so, once Subsidiary A enter the information of one bank-accepted bill into its own system, the Subsidiary B can also reuse the same information directly without repeated imputing. Hence, the routine of bank-accepted bill transfer among subsidiaries was simplified.

Routine Reconfiguration Brought by Training Policies

In addition to internal job rotation and internal collaboration, Wanhua's efforts to cultivate generalist can be also found in its distinct employee training policies: the company tends to provide specialist trainings to employees from a very broad scale. The company does not only offer internal trainings, such as IT training for staffs with diverse backgrounds, but also offers external training. For instance, before the company started its ERP implementation, the company first invented 13 staff to attend the training provided by SAP. Among all the attendants, only half of them were selected from the IT Department, while the rest half came from other departments, such as Finance Department, Production Department, etc.

Another example of such training is sending employees to pursue a masters degree on accounting. In 2010, Wanhua sent about 45 employees to enroll a part-time Master of Professional Accounting (MPAcc) Program that lasted for 2–3 years. It is no surprising for financial staff with relevant backgrounds to pursue an accounting master. However, among all the attendants, about 80% of them were staff from Marketing Department, Procurement Department, IT Department, etc., with no prior accounting or finance-related knowledge background.

Ms. Wang was one graduate of such MPAcc Program. She was in charge of the logistic work for the international orders under the Marketing Department. The core routine of her job is the product exportation routine.

In particular, this routine is generally designed as following: After the sales staff get an order from clients, the logistic staff will inform the Production Department to get the goods prepared, book cargo space for this order accordingly, and declare the good exportation details to the custom. Meanwhile, they will wait for the customers to send the Letter of Credit (L/C), which is a document issued by a bank to guarantee the payment from the client to Wanhua provided certain documents have been presented to the bank. After getting both the approval from the custom and confirmation of the payment from the clients, the logistic staff will arrange sufficient vehicles, then dispatch the goods from the warehouse to the cargo ship in order to complete the goods delivery. The shipping invoice will also send to clients for their reference. Finally, the logistic staffs will present required documents, including the shipping invoice, for payment from the bank. It usually takes about one month to complete the whole routine.

Although the product exportation routine is quite a standard routine with established arrangement, the implementation of Wanhua's ERP in 2008 still revised the particulars in completing this routine. Some of the changes are just about tools used to complete the routine. For instance, all the activities were recorded and managed via ERP instead of paper, and much internal communication can be conducted via ERP system virtually instead of via face-to-face communication. Some are more complicated. For instance, in terms of how to confirm the payment from the client, in the past, the logistic staff only need to confirm the payment once they received the L/C by themselves, then dispatch the goods directly. But now the ERP system requires the logistic staff to bring the L/C to the Finance Department. And only after getting approval from financial staff could they dispatch the goods.

For Ms. Wang, a senior staff who knew product exportation clearly, the change on dealing with L/C actually bothered her a lot, as she recalled: "we felt this (bringing the L/C to Finance Department for approval) brought us new troubles, and increased our working load meaninglessly." She had to follow the ERP reluctantly, but she had not been at her best to corporate with financial staffs and get things done smoothly. Such issue was a common challenge in the organization, as mentioned by another manager: "When we didn't have an ERP system, our staffs need to contact other departments very frequently, and acquire sufficient relevant knowledge of these departments to ensure that everything is done correctly. But now, since the ERP has articulated every step to do for our staff, they probably know little about other departments, [which inhibits our staff from utilizing knowledge from different domains]."

Ms. Wang's attitude towards such change gradually shifted after attending the MPAcc Program. By acquiring knowledge on accounting, Ms. Wang learnt a new perspective to understand what she was expected to do in product exportation routine: The financial staff want to verify the L/C carefully, so that it is ensured that the payment is secured. Just as she introduced: "After understanding accounting knowledge, you know this (bringing the L/C to Finance Department for approval) is designed for risk control. We can better understand why our financial staff ask for such action now."

Such improved understanding also led to better performance, as Ms. Wang summarized: "A better understanding about finance and accounting helps my work. I can better understand the policies and actions required by the Finance Department ... so that our communication with Finance Department becomes smoother [and response to them better], especially in terms of risk management, internal control ..."

References

Merchant Research & Consulting Ltd. Methylene Di-P-Phenylene Isocyanate (MDI): 2014 World Market Outlook and Forecast up to 2018, 2014. (available online at http://mcgroup.co.uk/researches/methylene-di-p-phenylene-isocyanate-mdi, last retrieved on 20 March 2014).

Wikipedia: The free encyclopedia. List of polyurethane applications, 2014. (available online at http://en.wikipedia.org/wiki/List_of_polyurethane_applications, last retrieved on 20 March 2014).

Discussion Questions

1. What are the key challenges in reconfiguring the organizational routines in advancing the company?
2. What are the key activities enacted in Wanhua's organizational transformation?

3. Do you agree with Wanhua's top management's ideas in resolving the company's challenges? What are the advantages and potential drawbacks of doing so?

4. What are some of the lessons learned from the success of Wanhua's routine reconfiguration that can be replicated after a company's ERP implementation?

15

Beijing Esky Technology

Taohua Ouyang, Hui Wang and Miao Cui

On May 27, 2010, Yu Huang, the founder of Beijing Esky Science & Technology Co., Ltd. (Esky) visited Nan Xue, the chairman of Hdc Software Co., Ltd. (Hdc). Straight to the point, Huang declared his purposes, "as Esky's bank loans and some other loans are due, I want to borrow RMB3 million from Hdc. I have no other choice."

Xue was astonished, "What? 3 million!" He hesitated for a moment and then said, "I have no intent to embarrass you. However, Hdc is a listed company. Our financial audit is very strict. What guarantee can you offer? The guarantee must be real estate. And its market value should be more than 3 million. We do not want to bear any financial risk."

Huang smiled bitterly. The only valuable thing he had was his apartment. Unfortunately, it had already been mortgaged to a bank. He had no idea how to answer Xue's question. Suddenly, the office phone rang. And Xue picked up the phone and talked to someone on the other side. It gave Huang a second to figure out the solution. First, only Hdc could save Esky. Second, to cooperate with Hdc, he had to ask for permission from Hong Kong Vito Science & Technology Co., Ltd. (Vito), a large shareholder of Esky. Several days ago, Vito reluctantly agreed on his proposal that by using Huang's apartment as the mortgage, if Esky could pay back

RMB8 million in 4 years, Vito would quit from Esky. However, the apartment had been already mortgaged to a bank last year to meet Esky's urgent needs. Therefore, to make the cooperation agreement with Hdc, Huang had to redeem his apartment from the bank. By now, only Hdc could offer him RMB3 million to redeem the apartment. This was the purpose of his visit. But to his surprise, Xue also asked him to mortgage his apartment. How could he figure out a solution?

To be honest, Huang quite understood Xue's requirements. Xue and he were merely business partners. He really appreciated Xue for his proposal of cooperation with Esky when Esky was in trouble. Xue's requirements were understandable as Esky's ownership structure was complex. Not to mention, RMB3 million was a large amount of money.

"Think it over. This is my best offer!" Xue stared at Huang after hanging up. "Thank you, Xue. I will think it over and visit you later." Huang pretended to be easy, said goodbye to Xue and then left the office.

Xue looked at Huang's back. He liked this young man since Huang reminded him of his own younger years. No matter in which situation, both of them were optimistic and confident. However, Xue could tell anxiety and helplessness from his eyes. It made Xue wonder what kind of difficulties he was facing. It was not a difficulty, but a hard knot.

From Hardware to Software

The First Pot of Gold

It was in August 2005. At that time, Huang served as a VIP customer sales manager in Beijing Shenwei Techonology Co., Ltd. (Shenwei). One day he quarreled with the sales president as they had different opinions on market development. In the last three years, Huang was committed to sales to telecommunication enterprises and was the most successful sales manager in the company. He insisted that Shenwei focussed on the telecommunication industry as there was still a huge potential in the industry. Different from Huang's opinion, the sales president asked Huang to explore new customers in other industries, such as financial industry and government, to open up new market for Shenwei. He further emphasized that this was in line with the corporate strategy, and Huang and other team members should obey the company's decision. It deepened Huang's feeling of being bound. He knew it was because he worked for others, not for himself. For a long time, he had a dream of starting his own business. Several years ago, he just graduated from the college and had no money to fulfill his dream. But now, he owned both money and energy. Why not start his own business?

Huang discussed his idea with two fellows, Rui Zhang, a sales staff and Hua Jiang, a pre-sales staff. Zhang and Jiang worked in Huang's team for the past two years and become Huang's close friends. When Huang told them he planned to leave Shenwei and start his own business, both Zhang and Jiang expressed their approval and desire to follow Huang. Shortly, the three submitted their resignation to Shenwei and left the company.

In September 2005, Huang scraped together RMB500,000 and set up Esky. He owned 60% equity stake. Zhang and Jiang did not invest any money. Huang gave them 20% equity stake respectively. At that time, Esky, who had only five employees, mainly sold bar code equipment and consumables to telecommunication enterprises. Besides three shareholders, the other two employees were Hui Zhang, in charge of Esky's financial issues and Chen, in charge of business.

Esky was lucky. In 2005, telecommunications enterprises fell over one another to construct information systems. Information management of fixed assets was a part of the construction. And the first step of information management of fixed assets was to make an inventory of fixed assets. And then information would be imported into a corresponding database and be embedded into ERP. Hence, there were huge demands to bar code equipment and consumables. Esky seized the opportunity to develop the market. Due to high-quality customers and the hard work, from September 2005 to the end of 2006, Esky's sales revenue reached RMB15 million. Esky survived the hardest period. Zhang and Jiang, in charge of the sales center and the technology center became the backbone of Esky.

Turned to the Software Industry

Although Esky was successful, Huang believed that demands for bar code equipment would not last for long as more and more telecommunication enterprises finished fixed asset inventory establishment. What should Esky do to cope with the situation? It troubled Huang and his team. They discussed this issue many times. However, they still could not find the way.

Fortunately, a skilled worker's idea enlightened Huang. The worker was responsible for assembling equipment for customers. He found that the equipment did not facilitate customers' asset management as expected as there was lack of correlation between the purchased ERP from foreign companies and the equipment. Asset information could not be imported to ERP directly so all these work had to be done manually. It was a time-consuming job due to the huge amount of information. Customers always complained that the equipment did not reduce workload, but rather increased the workload. When Huang learnt these, he began to visit customers. The feedback was exactly the same as the worker told him. To his surprise, when he visited Hebei Branch of China Mobile, after complaining the inefficiency of the equipment, a manager sighed, "I hope there is supporting software! We will definitely purchase it if is available." The words made Huang excited. His experiences told him that this was the direction for Esky.

The next day, Huang and several other skilled workers visited Hebei Branch of China Mobile again. They reached an agreement to develop fixed asset management software for telecommunication industry after deep discussion and field research. Later, Huang signed a fixed asset management project contract with Hebei Branch of China Mobile worthy of RMB3.2 million in which RMB1.2 million was used to purchase software and RMB2 million was used to purchase hardware. Since then, Esky began to expand the technical team and look for other projects. By the end of June 2007, Esky gained contracts of RMB12 million from 4 provincial branches of China Mobile. Software accounted for 1/3 of the projects. Esky successfully transferred from an equipment supplier to a software developer.

Differences of Profit Distribution

The success brought troubles to Esky at the same time. In a board meeting in early 2007, entrepreneurial team members raised different opinions about shareholder dividends. Huang insisted on maintaining enough capital and distributing less dividends to support Esky's future development. He further explained that software projects needed continuous investment to ensure sustainable development, and proposed that the 3/4 of profits in 2006 should be maintained. However, Zhang and Jiang insisted that more dividends were the best choice. Zhang claimed that although Esky was successful in recent years, demands for hardware would decrease, and the software market was full of uncertainties. Therefore, given that Esky had idle funds, improving shareholders' life quality should be given priority. The underlying reason for their hard work was to improve their families' life quality. Jiang further proposed that each shareholder should be distributed enough money to pay off home and car loans. Then idle funds could be invested in Esky.

Huang was on fire after hearing the two shareholders' opinions, "If you only desire to live a comfortable life, why you left Shenwei? Esky is our baby. You guys even do not believe her, how can she gain a promising future? Why you only consider your own life? How about other employees?"

Then Huang emphasized three points. First, he set up Esky for not only earning money. The most important thing was to build a successful and sustainable career. Second, as navigators, they should have enough confidence in Esky's success and its future. All the decisions should be made in line with Esky's future development. This was the basic line for Esky's further success. Third, Esky should act as a responsible company. Shareholders could not only consider their own interests. To lead all the employees to a better life was his goal and responsibility. At his insistence, all the board members agreed on the more retained earning proposal. And finally, Esky retained 1.5 million of the total 2 million profits in 2006. Only 0.5 million was used to distribute dividends.

However, the relationship between the three shareholders experienced unspeakable changes after the board meeting. It seemed that Zhang and Jiang were more complaining to Huang. All the decisions were in line with Huang's proposals. The previous fierce brawl disappeared. Huang could tell the changes. However, the young man thought this was due to his enhanced prestige and leadership. He had little time to investigate the reason as Esky was busy conducting several software development projects and the number of employees increased from 6 to more than 20.

Huang committed most of his time and energy to cope with the increasingly complex management jobs. And he still believed that their relationship was as close as brothers. It was inevitable that Huang neglected communication with Zhang and Jiang.

Lack of Capital and Looked for Investors

Esky gained reputation in the software development market and contracts from several other customers. However, as software development was labor-consuming and had a long project cycle and slow capital flow, Esky was lacking in funds and needed to look for new investors. In June 2007, by a friend's introduction, Huang met Sheng Wu, the chairman of Vito, a famous IT service company located in Hong Kong. At that time, Vito was intending to open up the Chinese mainland market. Wu was optimistic to Esky's development and willing to invest in Esky.

In July, Esky invited the CFO of every branch of China Mobile and many mass media to attend the launch conference for its fixed asset management software in Beidaihe City of Hebei Province. Then SHIYI became a famous fixed asset management software brand in the telecommunication industry. Esky was well known by telecommunication enterprises. Wu attended the conference, which made him determined to invest in Esky.

Separation and Survival Crisis

If Esky could grow on the right track, then the launch conference would pave the way for her further development and undoubtedly became an important milestone in its history. However, the seeming prosperity of the company made Huang neglect the internal risks.

Betrayal

After the Beidaihe conference, the north China market gradually got on the right track. However, the south China market did not improve. Huang was optimistic about the VP of marketing in charge of the south China market and intended to promote him. Therefore, he decided to stay for a while in Guangzhou to help the VP of marketing to open up the south China market and asked Zhang and Jiang to take charge of the Beijing headquarters business. However, beyond his imagination, a nightmare was waiting for him a month later.

The 3 million-project developed for Hebei Branch of China Mobile was almost finished. Hardware, with payment on Esky's account, was delivered to the customer. The software was about to finish after a 5-month development by 6 skilled programmers. Receivables were due in August 2007. So Huang asked Zhang, who was in charge of the project, to deal with the corresponding issues. And Zhang promised. He told Zhang that the customer would pay off in one week. In the following week, Huang did not much bother about the receivables. However, a week later, to his surprise, Huang noticed that the receivables did not arrive. So he called Zhang. Nobody replied the phone. He decided to directly enquire the customer about the debts. To his surprise, he found an unbelievable secret.

The Heibei Branch revealed that they had paid off at the end of August. They gave the money to Beijing Essky (Essky) authorized by Esky. The RMB3 million were transferred to a company that Huang had never heard of. And Essky only differed by one alphabet "s" from Esky. He was quite shocked and struggled to pull himself together. Huang searched on the Internet and found that Essky was founded in February 2007 and that the shareholders were Zhang and Jiang, who owned 50% equity stake respectively. Suddenly, he knew the truth. What a well-furnished scam! Huang felt like falling into an ice hole though the weather in Guangzhou was sweltering. He decided to fly back to Beijing immediately as the situation could not be worse anymore.

Negotiation and Separation

When arrived in Beijing, Huang met Zhang and Jiang. He held back his rage and faced them with a gentle state of mind to investigate the underlying reasons and to protect their friendship and Esky's development. After a night long talk, finally he knew the truth.

The bar code equipment market was promising in these two years. And Esky earned a large amount of money in 2006. However, Huang only focused on the future development and neglected shareholders' interests.

Zhang and Jiang worked very hard, but got only a few dividends. After the board meeting held in early 2007, they planned to run their own business. As Esky had gained good reputation in telecommunication industry and accumulated rich customer resources, they came up with an idea to set up a new company with a similar name. Their initial plan was to take use of Esky's reputation and steal some customers to facilitate Essky to get on the right track and then withdrew shares from Esky. They never thought that Esky won many software projects in recent years and was in lack of money. Therefore, even if they withdrew shares, they could not receive money immediately. Under this situation, they chose to take the risk and imitate Esky to dun Hebei Branch for the receivables. In the end of the talk, Zhang and Jiang proposed that they were willing to hand out the 40% shares of Esky they held. And the condition was that Huang gave up calling to account given that they contributed a lot to Esky in these years.

Huang did not agree on Zhang and Jiang's proposal that night. After the talk, he stayed in his office and fell into deep thought. In his opinion, Zhang and Jiang must withdraw from Esky. However, the results made him feel like being betrayed. Zhang was the most excellent sales personnel who ever trained and managed half of Esky's market. The most competent assistant would be soon transformed to a strong competitor. Jiang was in charge of the technical team in these years. If he decided to leave Esky, all the team members would choose to follow him. What left for Esky then? What came to his mind was legal recourse. Subcontract with permission violated laws. Huang could choose taking use of legal weapons to protect Esky's interests. However, he denied the idea immediately. He hated initiating legal proceedings. It was too hardhearted.

He had his own reasons. First, he had to admit that Esky's corporate system was imperfect and left them an opportunity. Besides, Hebei Branch was involved in the issue. If Esky initiated legal proceeding, the customer would be implicated. And this must have a negative effect on Esky's collaboration with Hebei Branch in the future. Second, Huang cherished Vito's investment. It was important to Esky's future development. To win Vito's investment intentions was not an easy thing. The legal proceeding might influence Vito's intention. Third, even if Esky won the case, Zhang and Jiang would leave the company. Their shares had to be bought out. According to Vito, Esky was evaluated as a RMB20 million company. Therefore, using 3 million to purchase 40% shares was a good price. Fourth, what mattered most was that although Zhang and Jiang damaged Esky's interests, they contributed a lot to the company and were close friends of Huang. He did not want to meet them in court.

Huang decided to negotiate with Zhang and Jiang. Finally, after a week long negotiation, they reached an agreement. Firstly, Huang bought back the 40% shares held by Zhang and Jiang and would never hold them accountable. Secondly, to protect the Esky brand, Essky would be renamed as Esuee and could no longer use SHIYI. Thirdly, Esky and Esuee signed a contract to divide market. Esky would cover 2/3 of the Chinese market.

After signing the contract, 12 sales and technical staff followed Zhang and Jiang to leave Esky. Only 10 persons chose to stay in Esky, including Huang, Hui Zhang, 4 technical interns and 4 logistics personnel. That night, Huang stayed up the whole night.

"We never reached agreement on Esky's strategy. It just seems we made agreement. However, actually, the lack of communication and my strong personality resulted in my failure."

The separation brought many troubles to Esky. What troubled most was the 3 million lost. The 3 million meant a lot of things to Esky.

Magnet and Ride out of the Storm

Zhang and Jiang's withdrawal made Esky's situation worse. Although Esky owned tens of millions of receivables, it could not be transferred to Esky according to contracts due to China Mobile's complex payment procedures. Esky could only receive the next receivables, RMB4 million, 3 months later. However, several urgent accounts payable was due. Especially, a 2.18 million accounts payable of Cosco was dunned. Unfortunately, the amount of the total company carrying plus Huang's saving was less than 500,000. Huang suffered from losing the trust of Cosco.

Cosco was the most important supplier of Esky. More than 95% hardware was provided by Cosco, who played an important role in Esky's growth. It was mainly because of Cosco that Esky could survive from the fierce competition among China Mobile's bar code equipment suppliers, as Esky lacked both capital and ties. Cosco had been supporting and caring Esky, whose purchases was less than 1% of its revenues, by offering preferential prices, advanced technologies, high-quality equipment, steady and short delivery cycle, and 2-month payment period, double of industry practices, in these two years. The preferential was rendered by Ming Chen, a VP of marketing at Cosco. Huang described Chen as one of the most important magnets in his life.

Huang met Chen when he worked in Shenwei. Chen's impression to Huang was not his excellent performance, but his surprising behavior. At that time, Shenwei's sales personnel were responsible for looking for both customers and suppliers. Shenwei executed contracts only after sales personnel signed contracts with both customers and suppliers. Besides, to avoid risks, Shenwei paid suppliers only after receiving customers' payment. In this way, suppliers were risk-takers of Shenwei. As a sales manager of Shenwei, Huang signed many purchase contracts with Cosco. However, among these contracts, Shenwei refused to pay off Cosco because she did not receive her customers' payment several times. Actually, delay in payment was quite normal in the industry. However, to Chen's surprise, every time, when there was a delayed payment, Huang paid off Cosco by using his own savings. Then, Huang entered Shenwei only a few months and had become the "best sales" in the company. Huang analyzed the reasons to Chen honestly. On one hand, he was confident with his customers. And on the other hand, given payment due was set in contract, payment should be encashed according to contracts. It paved the way for long-term and pleasant cooperation. Huang's action and words impressed Chen. From then on, Chen took extra care about him.

Facing the 2.18 million accounts payable, Huang sighed deeply. He had no idea how Chen would look on him. Having no choice, Huang had to visit Chen and told him the truth. Chen said he quite understood his difficulties and led Huang to meet the CEO of Cosco. Withstanding the pressure, Chen got the CEO's permission to extend the payment deadline for 3 months. During this period, Cosco kept supplying equipment to Esky. And Chen lent 500,000 of his own saving to Huang to relieve Esky's funding pressures.

Eventually, Esky survived the crisis due to the persistence of Huang and the other employees as well as the supporting from Cosco. Later, Huang unreservedly told Wu what happened. Wu was moved by Huang's honesty and tolerance and expressed his investment intention again. However, Wu was a businessman and proposed a half-year-probation. If Esky could operate without any influence of the crisis, then he would invest in Esky.

Shares and A Talent

Huang was not influenced by the frustration. On the contrary, he became stronger. To meet the half-year-probation requirements, he visited customers around the country to win more contracts and was always on business trips. Hence, he needed a person to be in charge of the Beijing headquarters. The desired one was a person with rich working experiences and contacts in the industry, and who is capable of attracting talents and wholeheartedly managing Esky. And this person must be a stranger!

Accidently, Huang read an interview of Feng Wan, a project manager of Teleyingke Beijing Co., Ltd. (TYK), the strongest competitor of Esky, in a business magazine. Wan's unique ideas of management and rich experiences attracted Huang. He knew Wan was the guy he was looking for.

One day, Huang visited Wan. Through the talk, he could tell that Wan felt unsuccessful in TYK. Wan had studied and worked in Australia for many years. He joined in TYK in 2003 and was a veteran in the company. In these years, he contributed a lot for TYK. However, he felt unsatisfied with his career as the Hong Kong headquarters did not believe in Chinese mainland employees and sent Hong Kong local employees to TYK to take senior offices. Wan and other mainland employees had no opportunity to get promotion. His knowledge, skill and energy were wasted.

On the contrary, Huang cherished Wan. However, Esky could not offer enough salary to attract Wan. But Huang thought shares and management rights might have more attraction to Wan.

Huang explained Esky's situation to Wan and promised that if Wan could join in Esky, he was confident that Esky would win Vito's investment half a year later. Huang further told Wan that he'd like to render Wan management rights and some voluntary shares. When Esky received the investment, Wan could choose to sell the shares and receive the corresponding money. Wan was attracted by Huang's offer. He further recommended Shi Liao to Huang. Liao once was a student of Wan and at that time was a core technical staff in his team.

A month later, Wan and Liao joined Esky. Wan became the CEO of Esky and owned Esky's 30% equity stake. Liao became the pre-sales president of Esky and owned 20% equity stake.

Learning from the previous lessons, before signing the equity transfer contract, Huang signed another contract with Wan and Liao. According to the contract, Huang would transfer 50% equity stake to Wan and Liao. They would work in Esky no less than 3 years from October 1, 2007. If Wan and Liao left Esky in 3 years or required to sell the shares, they had to return the shares to Huang voluntarily.

After Wan and Liao joined Esky, Huang was expecting for Esky's promising future.

Vito's Investment and Esky's Expansion

Gambling, Survival, and Listing

Since October 2007, Huang and his management team did their utmost to lead Esky from a wasteland to a peak. Esky won contracts from China Mobile, accounting for 1/3 of its fixed asset management and financial management systems. There were totally more than 40 employees in the company. However, Esky's HR cost increased sharply as she emphasized attracting talents. Fund shortage always accompanied Esky and negatively affected her development, even survival.

Luckily, Wan and Liao's joining built a shining management team for Esky. After several negotiations, Wu agreed to invest in Esky and signed an agreement on gambling with Esky on May 20, 2008. According to the agreement, Vito would buy Esky's 60% equity stake with RMB15 million. 50% of the 15 million would be paid in three years. And the other 50% was Vito's IPO when listing. Esky ensured that in the following 3 years, that was 2008, 2009 and 2010, after-tax profits were no less than RMB7, 8, and 10 million respectively. Vito promised providing liquidity according to budget and listing before December 31, 2010. The original shareholders could independently operate and manage Esky for at least 5 years.

After signing the contract, Vito transferred the 1st equity transfer fund, 3 million, to Esky's original shareholders accordingly. Besides,

Esky decided to increase the registered capital to 5 million. Vito invested 2.7 million according to the percentage of shares.

Vito's investment changed Esky's ownership structure. Vito owned 60% (According to the contract, Vito's shares would reach 60% after 3 years). Huang owned 20% and took the executive director office. Wan, the CEO., owned 12%. And Liao, the pre-sales president, owned 8%.

For the Growth of Esky

After receiving the 3 million from Vito, Huang distributed 900 thousand and 600 thousand to Wan and Liao respectively according to their percentages of shares. And Wan and Liao's monthly salary increased from 10 thousand to 30 thousand and 25 thousand respectively. Since then, Esky entered a fast growth period.

The organizational structure and the management system became more mature. Management team members cooperated with each other quite well. Wan was called "Spiritual Leader" of Esky due to his unique charisma. When recalled Wan of the year, older employees described him as "He was eloquent and humorous. His speeches were full of passion. Everyone enjoyed his speech and wanted to follow him. He always accepted rewards on behalf of Esky. Some business journalists interviewed him. You can find the reports on the Internet."

Wan's impressive resume and his eloquence facilitated Esky's success in dealing with external issues. At the same time, Huang was a master hand at winning contracts. Before receiving Vito's investment, Esky had given up many large contracts due to fund shortage. The investment relieved Huang's anxiety. The corporate strategy emphasized more on expansion. And the company signed more than 10 contracts, totally 40 million, with China Mobile. The number of its employees increased to 80. Esky became one of the most competitive enterprises in the industry, except for IBM and TYK.

The Financial Crisis

In 2008, the global financial crisis hit the world economies. Vito suffered greatly and could not provide capital according to Esky's budget.

Unfortunately, Esky was carrying out several large-scale software projects at the same time. These projects had to be completed in stages. Only 10% of the total amount was paid after corresponding stage acceptance check as customers were very strong. Acceptance check was very strict and took several months. It meant that Esky had to invest large amounts of money and technical and managerial staff to these projects in the beginning stage. Therefore, Esky was in deficit in the 1st stage, could balance its payment in the 2nd stage, and began to make profit in the 3rd stage. However, most of the 20 projects under construction were in the 1st stage. The demand of large amount of money made Esky fall into the capital crisis again.

Huang talked with Wu many times. He hoped that Vito would keep its promise to provide enough money to support Esky's operation. He even proposed that Esky would like to loan from Vito. However, Wu refused to provide any money.

Unfortunately, Esky's hardware business was devastated. Since 2009, China Mobile changed its hardware purchase policy. The headquarters were in charge of the unified procurement, rather than decentralized procurement by branches. The new policy set very strict standards for suppliers' qualification and financial capacity. It was a disaster for Esky and other small-scale suppliers and broke Esky's plan to ease the financial strain by hardware business.

Shrinkage and Subsistence

Find Ways to Live

After Wu refused his proposal, Huang knew that Esky had to rescue herself. In 2009, Esky stopped to expand and began to shrink and subcontract some projects.

To save cost, Huang proposed that three shareholders' monthly salary should be decreased to RMB3,000 since March 2009. And the differences would be made up if Esky survived the financial crisis. Wan and Liao expressed their understanding towards Huang's proposal. However, Liao further announced that nobody could make a living with 3,000 in Beijing. After hearing that, Wan persuaded him. And finally, Liao agreed on Huang's proposal.

At the same time, Huang invested the RMB1.5 million, distributed from Vito's equity transfer, and all his savings to Esky. In July 2009, he mortgaged his apartment to a bank for loans. Eventually, Esky survived in 2009.

Another Separation

It seems that Liao was still discontent with the salary decrease. He always raised objections to Huang's proposal in the senior manager meeting. Once he publicly expressed that he could not finish the job after Huang assigned tasks. Huang immediately got angry and bellowed to Liao, "If you can't, get out of Esky." And finally, Liao was demoted on the spot. After that, Wan acted as a peacemaker between Huang and Liao. However, Wan still felt ashamed as Liao was his student. The relationship among three shareholders underwent subtle changes.

In the end of 2009, Wan asked Huang to restore his salary as he was facing pressures of wedding and housing. But Huang refused and insisted that shareholders should follow the low-paying policy. Wan was a sensitive young man. After Huang refused his requirement, he never asked for it again. Wan felt despair in Esky. His knowledge, skill and energy were wasted again.

He seldom went on duty except for attending important meetings, and found a part time job outside. Huang listened to the news and connived as he could understand Wan's situation.

Esky's financial crisis was not eased in 2010. Vito refused to pay the 2nd equity transfer fund to Esky using "Esky's revenue in 2009 did not pass the minimum standard" as the pretext. Although Huang thought it was ridiculous, he did not quarrel with Wu as he appreciated Vito's help in 2008 and looked forward to Vito's recovery.

On April 1, 2010, Wan submitted his resignation to Huang and told him he would join in a real estate company with annual salary of RMB800,000. Huang did not detain him. Neither of them mentioned the divestment and 3 year timeline issue in the contract. Huang understood Wan's reason. His leaving was for a living. So he did not mention the contract.

Looking for Investment

After Wan's leave, Esky's situation became worse. Huang invested everything he had to the company and had nothing else to invest. He even mocking himself that "I'm poorer than any normal employee." Huang had no choice but to look for new investment.

However, it was not an easy thing for Esky. On one hand, the ownership structure was complex. According to the contract, Vito owned 60% of Esky's equity stake, however, the company did not pay for the total equity transfer fund and its going public seemed hopeless. On the other hand, different shareholders had different goals. Everyone pursued for his own interests. It was harmful to Esky's development.

Wan, Liao and Wu agreed to sell Esky. Wu wanted his money back, at least to balance the 5.7 million investment. Wan and Liao hoped to receive some money by selling their shares. However, Huang had different opinions. He viewed Esky as a part of his life and was worried about suspending wages, stopping projects and losing customers and his apartment, which had already been mortgaged to a bank. He urgently needed a new investor. Huang was still confident with Esky. Esky had projects and skilled staff. He only needed money to survive the crisis. However, he knew that to attract a new investor was difficult, so he had to make the potential investor feel confident with Esky. How difficult the job was!

Teamsun

On April 8, 2010, Huang met Weihang Wang, the CEO of Beijing Teamsun Technology Co., Ltd. (Teamsun). Teamsun, an IT service supplier, set up in 1998, successfully went public in 2004. Wang admired Huang's market developing capacity and his contribution to Esky's reputation and expressed his intention to invest in Esky. However, to Huang's surprise, in the formal negotiation, the representative of Teamsun announced they were not interested in Esky, but hoped Huang could bring Esky's core staff to Teamsun. Huang did not accept Teamsun's proposal. He still wished that Teamsun could invest in Esky and Esky could maintain its independence. The two sides did not make any agreement in the negotiation. On that day, only Huang and Liao attended the negotiation.

Two days later, Huang received a phone call from Wang. Wang said that today he called him as a friend. He received an SMS with the signature of an employee of Esky. The main content of the SMS was that Esky was valueless to invest and Teamsun should not invest in Esky as Wan, the heart and soul and the most valuable person, had already left Esky. Wang further commented that Esky's ownership structure was too complex. It made the investment in Esky full of risk. Huang was shocked by the phone call. And he knew that the negotiation between Esky and Teamsun came to the end.

There were many questions in Huang's heart. Who sent the SMS? Why did he do this? Suddenly, he remembered Liao, the other one who attended the negotiation. He had many reasons to suspect Liao. Liao was the most likely person to describe Wan as the heart and soul of Esky. Besides, other employees had no idea about the negotiation. In addition, Huang knew that Liao was bottom-up minded. He was probably the subject of instigation. Huang felt very disappointed. However, there was no proof. He had to stay calm and collected. He harbored grudge against Wan and Liao and wanted to ask them to return the shares. However, he could not tell. Several times, words were on his tongue.

China.com

On April 15, 2010, introduced by Wu, Esky held an investment negotiation with China.com. China.com was one of the largest English portals in China, providing news, business information, learning materials, travel information, etc. In the negotiation, without Huang's permission, Wu announced that Vito wished to sell the 60% equity stake of Esky at the price of RMB6 million. Huang objected when he heard this and insisted that Vito did not own 60% shares. Finally, the negotiation ended in failure. And the relationship between Huang and Wu became worse.

Beyondsoft

On April 22, 2010, introduced by Wan, Esky held an acquisition talk with Beyondsoft. Beyondsoft, set up in 1995, was an IT service outsourcing company. It recognized Esky's value in the industry. However, after the negotiation representatives were aware of Esky's situation, they refused to take over Esky giving the reason that its ownership structure was too complex. The negotiation ended in failure again.

> *"The negotiation with Beyondsoft impressed me most as my wedding would be held in the next day. After receiving a SMS of refusal to takeover Esky, I made an appointment with the chairman immediately to meet in a café near his apartment at 8 pm. I took all the files. Our talk lasted to 11 pm. However, the result was not changed. I was in despair on the way to home. However, when I opened the door and saw the decoration in the house and my parents smile, suddenly I felt energetic and believed that Esky would be an excellent company in the future."*

Exhausted

Hdc

Huang felt tired and exhausted after several failed negotiations. On May 15, 2010, he communicated with Chen. After learning about Huang's difficulties, Chen introduced Jian Yang, one of his classmates at EMBA program at Cheung Kong Graduate School of Business and the CFO and the secretary of the board of Hdc, to Huang. Yang admired Huang and introduced him to Xue, the chairman, the next day.

Hdc, set up in 2001 and listed in August 2006, was committed to software development, information system integration, and information technology service. Xue felt Huang was like an old friend at the first sight as he had the same experiences with Huang. Both of them worked as a sales staff at the beginning of their career, run own business due to hate constraints, and believed in "good faith". Although Xue was 20 years older than Huang, they called each other "brother". And Xue agreed to invest in Esky.

Huang was an honest young man. He told Xue everything about Esky. Xue replied, "Esky's ownership structure was too complex. It made my investment risky." Then Xue proposed to set up a new company, funded by Hdc and managed by Huang. Huang and Hdc signed a contract on gambling, i.e., Huang exchanged certainty percentage of Hdc's shares with performance of the new company.

Huang knew that the offer was because of Xue's trust in him. After experiencing betrayal and difficulties in these years, he cherished Xue's recognition and trust. Huang expressed his willingness to accept Xue's offer. However, he also hoped Xue could give him some time to solve the remaining problems to avoid troubles to the new company.

After the meeting with Xue, Huang called Wu to express his appreciation to Vito and tell Wu his decision of cooperation with Hdc to avoid the bankruptcy of Esky. Huang further suggested that if Wu agreed on his proposal, he would pay 8 million to Vito in 4 years as the compensation of Vito's 5.7 million investment.

There was a moment of silence on each side of phone. Finally, Wu agreed and made an appointment with Huang to sign an agreement on May 25. Unfortunately, a tremendous misfortune was waiting for Huang.

A Hard Knot

In the morning of May 23, Zhang, the CFO of Esky, called Huang and told him the company was stolen and he had called policemen. Huang rushed to the office and found that the financial office was broken in and none was missing. Only Zhang's laptop was logged in by someone else. The drafted cooperation agreement with Huang was stored in the laptop. Huang was aware that he had to talk to Liao. However, when he called Liao, he found that Liao's phone was powered off.

The next day, Xue asked Huang to meet him at his office. He gave his cell phone to Huang to let him see the SMS. The SMS was sent by Wan. Wan told Xue that Wu was the largest shareholder of Esky. Huang had no right to represent Esky to discuss cooperation with Hdc. Wan suggested Xue to meet Wu to discuss the cooperation between the two companies. Finally, Xue asked Huang's opinion to deal with the issue. Huang thought it over for a while and said, "Let's meet together."

On May 25, Xue and Huang met Wu. Wu's opinion changed tremendously. He announced he owned 60% shares of Esky and was the largest shareholder. Wu further clarified his idea that if HUAGONG paid RMB8 million to buy out his shares, he would quit Esky.

Xue immediately rejected Wu's proposal and said Hdc never planned to cooperate with Esky. Who was the largest shareholder was the internal issue of Esky and had no business with Hdc.

Wu did not reach his goal in the meeting. His going back on his words inflamed Huang. Huang did not mince his words, "if you follow Wan and Liao's suggestion, Esky would go bankrupt. Then there is nothing you could gain."

Wu did not deny that he had ever met Wan and Liao. He could tell that Xue favored Huang and finally agreed to sign the "8 million in 4 years" agreement with Huang. However, he insisted on adding an additional condition that Huang mortgaged his apartment to him.

However, at that time, Huang's apartment had been mortgaged to a bank. He had no choice but to visit Xue to borrow RMB3 million to pay off the deferred payment and get back his apartment. Xue replied he could lend 3 million to Huang, but Huang had to mortgage his apartment.

Xue and Wu both ask him to mortgage his apartment. This was a hard knot for Huang.

Discussion Questions

1. What death factors did Esky encounter in the entrepreneurial process? Summarize the death factors that entrepreneurial enterprises may encounter and analyze the reasons.

2. Market opportunities promoted the creation and development of Esky. Why was the company able to seize market opportunities and why was it also confused by market opportunities and changes? What should start-ups do to not only be able to seize market opportunities but also to cope with market dynamics? Please investigate why market dynamics have profound effect on entrepreneurial enterprises' development?

3. The two successively formed executive teams of Esky were both from cooperation to collapse and brought devastating blow to the company. Why did executive team members choose to leave the company in the business slump and why did they also choose to leave the company when the company's future was promising? In conjunction with the case, please discuss how to set up executive teams and how to maintain the teams.

4. Esky hesitated to sign contracts with customers due to fund shortage in the beginning stage. However, after receiving Vito's investment, Esky entered into a high-speed growth period but still encountered fund shortage. Why did fund shortage always accompany Esky and other entrepreneurial enterprises and why does it have huge effects on start-ups?

5. There were several investment negotiations between Huang and potential investors. What kind of values did investors attach to? Why did the first three potential investors decide to give up and why did Hdc agree to invest in Esky?

6. If you were Huang, what you will do to cope with the hard knot?

16

Zhejiang Cancer Hospital (ZCH)

Say Yen Teoh and Xi Chen

Introduction

Over the last decade, China's health care industry has undergone a period of restructuring and reformation triggered by a series of new health care policies, especially the 3A Hospital Certification Health care Rating introduced by the government in April 2005. To qualify for the 3A rating, a hospital needed to earn at least 900 out of a possible 1000 points that comprise a comprehensive assessment of the hospital's medical-staff expertise, administration, equipment, health care-IT standards, and research performance (Hudong, 2011). The introduction of a 3A Hospital Certification Health care Rating, added competition and assessment pressure across hospitals.

The President of Zhejiang Cancer Hospital (ZCH) represented his hospital by attending a Zhejiang Medical Professional Board meeting. However, during the meeting, the ZCH — now one of the four leading cancer specialist hospitals in China — was cited by the Zhejiang board as being the poorest-performing hospital, with an obsolete Healthcare

Information System (HIS). As a president who takes pride in his hospital's performance, he was extremely surprised and felt challenged by the board. Immediately, he was convinced that he had to make a difference. To do so, his first step was to discuss this issue with the ZCH senior management before launching a thorough investigation of the hospital's HIS performance.

Industry Background

The health care system in China has its own characteristics with several challenges: The inefficient, poorly organized health care delivery-system is bloated in urban areas and threadbare in rural sectors; it lacks a professional ethic to protect the interests of patients and the quality of its services; China is a huge diverse region (Hsiao, 1995). According to the Research Report of the Chinese Hospital Information Development (Accenture, 2008), hospital information-dissemination in China can be categorized into four stages. First is the single-machine and single-user application stage of around 1980. The second is the system-application stage in the middle of the 1980s. The third refers to the use of the internet and a database that developed rapidly in the 1990s, which triggers a hospital information-dissemination need. In very recent years, the sense of urgency to implement a new health care IT system was triggered (Accenture, 2008), as it was seen as the key to resolving the uneven development between rich urban and poor rural areas, and the important role played by vertical programs. These are the two main issues related to the complexity of the health care system in this developing country (Braa *et al.*, 2007).

To comply with the latest introduction of new policies, many hospitals, including ZCH, accepted the challenge and joined the trend by taking the risk of implementing a seamless fully integrated health care system to improve hospital service and care for patients.

Hospital Background

ZCH was founded in 1963. It is located in the north–east part of Hangzhou, the capital city of Zhejiang Proinvce. This is one of the most prosperous provinces and lies on the east coast of China. With 50 years of history, it is one of the most successful hospitals specializing in cancer treatment in China, and for that reason it attracts millions of patients. Despite its clinical achievements, the hospital continues to receive many complaints from doctors, nurses, and patients in terms of its healthcare process efficiency, effectiveness, and medical-record accuracy and reliability.

To remain competitive, and to keep up with the industry 3A certification, ZCH invested RMB200 million to reform its HIS. The reformation of ZCH's HIS began in 2006. After 12 weeks and three days of continuous effort, a hospital-wide information system was implemented (Figures 1 and 2). It consists of three integrated health care information systems. These are (1) HIS, (2) Electronic Medical Records (EMR), and (3) Laboratory Information Systems (LIS).

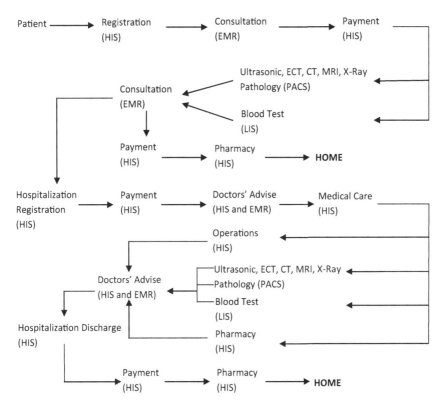

Figure 1. The Use of Three Integrated Healthcare Information Systems (HIS, EMR, and LIS) to Assist Patient Flow in ZCH.

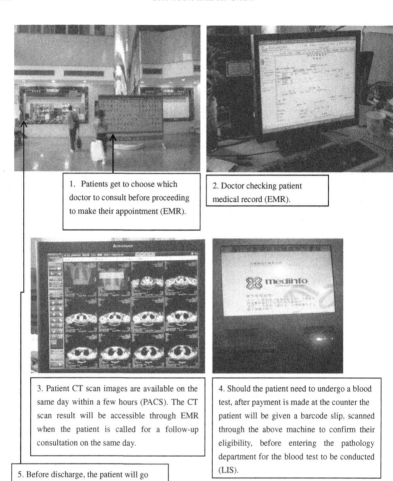

Figure 2. Picture Samples of the Use of Three Integrated Healthcare Information Systems (HIS, EMR, and LIS) Throughout a Patient's Visit to ZCH.

Currently, this hospital is using its fully fledged, integrated HIS to serve some 1,100 employees and 136 medical professors by making their jobs more efficient and effective. They treat approximately 1500 outpatients per day and in the order of 60,000 inpatients per year (Qebsoft, 2006).

We find that the system is rather powerful and has eased our workload tremendously. For example we now can copy and paste some standard prescriptions and diagnosis statements … it improves the efficiency of our work.

— A Medical Doctor.

This high-quality HIS enabled the hospital's expansion through having more sophisticated medical research, using new technologies in the fields of surgery, radiotherapy, chemotherapy, pathology, traditional medical therapy, intervention therapy, and biological treatments. Additionally, the hospital attracts much international collaboration and delivers remarkable progress on therapeutic efficacy and patient well-being.

Development of HIS Implementation — Identifying Needs (Early 2006)

The hospital began its HIS investigation by engaging an independent auditing group to review the performance of the IT department. Shortly after, the auditor shared her alarming feedback with the hospital's president:

"Instead of investigating the source of data inconsistency, they found out that the previous IT staff would (unethically) modify the raw data in the database to balance the financial accounts."

This feedback verified countless complaints about its poor IT support in terms of financial-accounting consistency, traceability, and medical-record accuracy and reliability. With the evidence gathered through the independent consultant, the hospital president called another urgent meeting with the Board of Directors for support and advice. Eventually, after thorough analysis, the hospital decided to reform its HIS and aimed to meet the 3A rating certification assessment that was due in mid-September 2006.

Responding to Needs (June 2006)

To reach the time target efficiently and effectively, ZCH management immediately reformed its IT governance by introducing a new approach — leadership monarchy.

If you need a speedy implementation and change, the leader must have strong governing power and decision-making power. As we all know, too many cooks would spoil the broth.

— ZCH President

Under the leadership-monarchy model, the president strategically revolutionized the hospital from its worst-performing area — the IT department — by painstakingly transferring the previous IT staff to IT vendors. He then introduced a new IT-governance process to establish tighter control guidelines — as to what had to be done, by whom, when, and how — to a group of enthusiastic IT staff. This group was led by a new Director of the Information Center (DIC), Ms. WANG Dingzhu. She has more than 20 years of nursing experience, and a vast knowledge of hospital management and clinical processes. Although she does not have an IT background, she tapped into her rich network in the field by inviting professors from Peking University to assist in the system-implementation planning. Acting as independent consultants and evaluators, this group of professors addressed the hospital's issue of a lack of staff expertise in this HIS-implementation project.

To minimize user resistance, the hospital president and other senior management attended all of the seminars that were held to prepare users for the new IT implementation. With the presence and strong support of senior management, staff members became enthusiastic.

After the announcement was made of this implementation, the president and a few selected IT-department representatives visited and learned from hospitals which had successfully implemented HIS. Upon returning from the field visits, the president made a unilateral decision to outsource this project and to enlist a renowned IT consultancy firm.

We were glad and pleased to know that the president did take others' lessons and success into consideration by outsourcing this project. We were totally lacking in experience and expertise of such a large and expensive integrated system implementation.

— An IT staff member

To ensure that the hospital selected the most reliable consultant, a stringent process of vendor selection was held. Various healthcare industry leaders demonstrated their IT prototypes to selected hospital representatives, and hundreds of vendor-selection surveys were issued to users, IT staff, and senior management. Eventually, Mediinfo was shortlisted for its expertise and sound reputation in the industry.

Taking the advantage of this being Mediinfo's first project in Hangzhou, the president strategically negotiated a special implementation price, and in exchange gave Mediinfo the privilege of advertising its involvement in this large-scale health care IT implementation.

Throughout this stage, ZCH introduced leadership-monarchy governance to achieve its internal efficiency through introducing new policies to manage changes in responding to its needs and goals.

Coordinating the Relationship and System Implementation (June to September 21, 2006)

To implement an integrated health care system within a few months of the due date for the 3A rating assessment, ZCH went into overdrive in June 2006. To govern better for responsive decision-making, the president maintained an active role, but the main driver for this phase was the joint effort between the Vendor Project Manager (PM) and the DIC.

> Adjustment for appropriate governance is crucial in this project, I have to analyze what's needed by the team constantly, and how I could better support them for speedy implementation, especially when the time is running out.
>
> — President, ZCH

A federal approach is designed to grant considerable autonomy and flexibility that speed up the decision-making process for the two professionals — the Vendor PM and DIC — with strong support from the president in this dynamic and demanding phase.

Encouraged by consistent support from the president, the DIC and Vendor PM were able to gain confidence to discuss and share their expertise and experiences openly in leading this project. The sanction from top management gave the newly joined Vendor PM the tenacity to shape the system-implementation planning and make critical suggestions in leading three groups of IT consultants (PACS, Mediinfo, and EMR) who came from diverse backgrounds.

There is barely sufficient time for orientation to welcome the newly joined IT consultants, as we have to integrate and implement all systems within one month; therefore, the only way is to encourage communication among staff. We tried our best to provide a friendly working environment for them, including using our lunch time to create more opportunities to come to know each other.

DIC Assistant

Another relationship-related issue was winning the cooperation of some of the hospital's doctors. Some rather conservative doctors were reluctant to adopt this new system that lead to more transparency and control in using accepted prescriptions that complied with Ministry of Health standards and policy. Fortunately, with continuous education, patient explanation, and strong reassurance from DIC and Vendor PM that the use of the new systems was not intended to deprive or challenge doctors' rights, the doctors eventually accepted the change.

Aside from overcoming relationship-related challenges, DIC and Vendor PM were further challenged by many system-related issues. One of the most challenging of these was to integrate the three systems which comprised the front-end systems to support clinical workflow for a seamless clinical service. However, due to intellectual property rights, neither EMR nor Mediinfo was willing to disclose their source code to enable the integration process to commence. After a prolonged stalemate, and pressured by time constraints, the president had to step in and resolve this by issuing an ultimatum. Once Mediinfo, the main contractor, capitulated by opening its healthcare-IT source code for EMR to integrate, the EMR team agreed to cooperate. With cooperation between the two companies, they subsequently won many contracts based on their record of accomplishment in ZCH.

We have done health care-IT implementation in more than 300 hospitals across China but we have never done integration with EMR. After the president stated his point clearly, as the main vendor of this project we had to give in to our customer's needs. In the end, we were pleasantly surprised by what we could achieve. This integration is a breakthrough for all of us.

Vendor PM

The efficient and effective resolution of complex and dynamic relationship and system-related issues was made possible by the application of adaptive IT governance for an agile approach in this phase.

Maneuvering Resources for System Go-Live (Mid-July to September 21, 2006)

With a track record of continuous success, DIC and Vendor PM eventually won trust from the president.

> In this phase, my involvement is minimal as they are now all on the right track and are able to navigate towards the set goal; therefore, all I do is provide support and encouragement.
>
> President

To govern better for agile implementation at this crucial stage, the IT-monarchy approach was adopted. The DIC and Vendor PM were able to make decisions to deal with changing situations with less concern about reporting and obtaining approval and consent from the president. The president played a supervisory and supportive role, with minimal intervention in this phase.

Empowered with full authority, the DIC could allocate resources and expedite matters so that the Vendor PM received all necessary support to meet the looming deadlines. First, the DIC analyzed the hospital's daily operational needs before merging her plan with the Vendor PM's plan and thus executed the parallel system migration and skills mapping for the system to go-live. Vendor PM quickly sourced and brought in people with the new required skills from the three vendors' headquarters (PACS, Mediinfo, and EMR) to complement the existing IT workforce across the hospital, and to support parallel system implementation.

> I'm also highly inspired by this hospital's working spirit. To support them, I have all my staff working in the hospital for a few days a week to keep up with the EMR system integration issue.
>
> EMR CEO

At the same time, DIC fully executed her authority to dictate departments' scheduled systems shutdowns and all required support and cooperation to go-live with the new systems.

> I have to make sure that when the system is down for migration, doctors are not consulting any patients. Accurate planning is crucial in the health care environment, especially as we have a 24-hour emergency department.
>
> DIC

Based on the DIC concerns, medical staff were told to make contingency plans, where carefully planned "workaround" processes were geared to handle any unintended difficulties arising from the changeover.

Within 24 hours, the new integrated health care IT was installed. System testing and maintenance were carried out immediately to monitor the stability of the new systems. Without further waste of time, medical and administrative staff were given on-the-job training. User feedback was collected during the training which was filtered by the DIC before sending for system customization, if required. Working side by side, technical experts from EMR and PACS were testing their source codes to synchronize system integration. To ensure round-the-clock implementation support, key stakeholders (five internal IT staff and six IT consultants, including the DIC and the Vendor PM) stayed in the hospital for the critical first month until all systems were fully integrated and implemented across the hospital.

> I'm very glad to be working with this IT HOD because she can always find ways to get the necessary support to make sure that we have enough manpower to run the parallel project implementation. More importantly, I'm very impressed with the culture of this hospital's staff, where they are willing to work extra hours, including staying in the hospital. I am impressed by them; I joined them by staying in the hospital for one month without going home.
>
> Vendor PM

In the fourth week, IBM, the third-party consultant came to assist ZCH in system migration. To ensure the success of the system migration (within a span of a few hours), the DIC and Vendor PM mobilized all of their available resources (about 30 staff) to assist the IBM consultants. Eventually, they managed to run the new system successfully at 6 A.M., the start of the hospital day. The implementation teams were on high alert for the first half of the day, before the project was declared a success and ready for the government's 3A rating assessment in three days.

Achievements and Recognitions (Late 2006 to Early 2007)

In just 12 weeks and three days, ZCH (Figure 3) successfully completed its health care-IT implementation, an outstanding achievement via the speedy adaptation of an IT-governance approach according to the needs of the project. The hospital was not only successfully awarded the 3A accreditation by the government, it was awarded the title of Demonstration Base of Health care IS Research and Development in Zhejiang Province (*Zhejiang Daily*, 2007). Its success and rapid HIS implementation has attracted presidents

Figure 3. Zhejiang Cancer Hospital Website.

Source: http://www.zchospital.com/cms/default.aspx.

and chief technology officers from other hospitals who visit ZCH from time to time to learn about its experience of HIS implementation (*Zhejiang Daily*, 2007).

References

Accenture. Chinese Hospital Information Development, China Hospital Association Information Management Committee Report, 2008.

Braa, J., Hanseth, O., Heywood, A., Mohammed, W., and Shaw, V. "Developing health information systems in developing countries: The flexible standards strategy," *MIS Quarterly* 2007, 381–402.

Hsiao, W. C. "The Chinese health care system: Lessons for other nations," *Social Science and Medicine*, (41:8) 1995, 1047–1055.

Hudong. (2011), 3A Rating Definition and Standard, viewed on 29 April (available online at http://www.hudong.com/wiki/%E4%B8%89%E7%BA%A7%E7%94%B2%E7%AD%89%E5%8C%BB%E9%99%A2).

Qebsoft Consulting Firm. Case study of ZCH successful HIS implementation, 2006. viewed on 20 April, 2011 (available online at http://www.qebsoft.com/cn/customers_1.asp).

Zhejiang Daily. A healthcare information system training base is established in Zhejiang cancer hospital, 2007. viewed on 5 May, 2011 (avaliable online at http://zjdaily.zjol.com.cn/html/2007-08/09/content_260459.htm).

Discussion Questions

1. Identify the business, technical, and relationship challenges encountered by this hospital throughout the system implementation.

2. Identify and discuss how the hospital sensed challenges and what they did in responding to challenges in every phase of the system implementation.

3. How many types of IT-governance approaches were applied to ensure agile implementation of the health care IT? What are the applied IT-governance approaches?

4. Do you agree with ZCH constant change on different types of IT-governance approaches used throughout the system implementation? In your opinion, what could possibly go wrong?

17

COFCO Group

Mao Mao

Industrial Background

Along with the rise of industrialization and service industries, China is a predominantly agricultural country with a large population. Agriculture and husbandry play important roles in the national economy. Still, the proportion of primary industry in national economic output has been continuously declined. In 2011, agricultural output accounted for 10.12% of GDP, down to the second lowest point in history. However, as the primary industry, agriculture is still a big issue related to people's livelihood in China.

Despite the decline in global economic development, as one of the traditional industries, the food processing industry has been less affected by the fluctuations of economic decline, presenting as a typical defensive sector. Thus, in the recent years (from 2003 to 2011), the major business income of the food processing industry has been in a steady upswing. Figure 1 shows that during the period, the rapid development of Chinese agriculture provides the food processing industry with rich and abundant raw materials. Coupled with the policy of expanding domestic demand and rigid demand, the food processing industry successfully shows rapid development. The growth rate of the major business income of the food

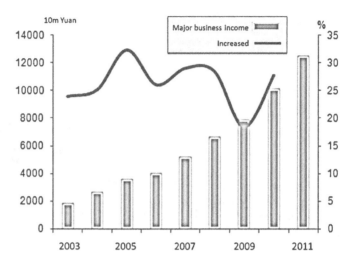

Figure 1. Trend of Major Business Income of Food Possessing Industry in China from 2003 to 2011.

Source: Development Research Center of the State Council.

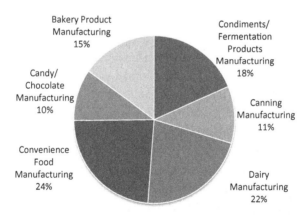

Figure 2. Total Output Value of Sub-Units of Food Processing Industry in 2011.

Source: Development Research Center of the State Council.

processing industry remained at 18–33% with a compound annual growth rate at 23.35%.

Also, in analyzing the sub-units in food processing industry, the pie chart in Figure 2 indicates that in 2011, convenience food manufacturing and dairy manufacturing represent the highest share in the industry (18.02% and 16.52%) with the growth rate at 40.8% and 22%. Among the 7 sub-units, convenience food manufacturing represents the fastest growth, which is 9% higher than the average growth in the industry.

Company Background

COFCO Group is currently one of the largest suppliers of diversified products and services in the agricultural products and food industry in China. COFCO primarily engages in food processing and food trading, including oilseed, wineries, beverages, confectionery, wheat, brewing material, rice, and biofuel. Since China's dairy scandal in 2008 — a food safety incident in China involving milk and infant formula and other food materials and components adulterated with melamine (see Branigan, 2008) — food security has become an issue of great concern, and incidents related to food quality have been widely reported throughout China. To guarantee the continuity and stability of food production and the total control of food quality along the production chain, COFCO is building a fully integrated value chain and thus requires the implementation of an integrated enterprise system along with the active participation of its subsidiaries. The subsidiary units are shown in Figure 3.

The integrated ES implementation project required high involvement from COFCO's major subsidiaries (the major subsidiaries we interviewed

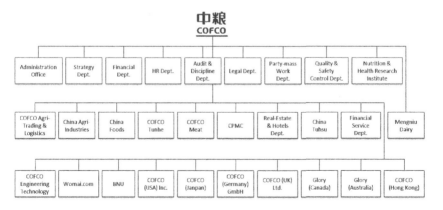

Figure 3. Organizational Structure of COFCO Group.

included COFCO Meat, China Foods, China Agri-Industries, COFCO Tunhe, and Womai.com). However, during the ES pre-implementation, diverse discrepancies remained among these subsidiaries. These discrepancies derived from various aspects of the subsidiaries such as business dynamisms, IT resources, and capability. To systematically and comparably reveal the discrepancies within COFCO subsidiaries, we adapt the dimensions from self-discrepancy theory to indicate the current states of four subsidiaries (Womai.com, COFCO Tunhe, China Foods, and COFCO Meat).

Requirements from the Headquarters

In COFCO Group, as a traditional Chinese state-owned corporation, headquarters makes the final decisions for enacting general strategy in the subsidiaries. Under these circumstances, the ought state of each subsidiary can be viewed as the requirements from COFCO headquarters. Generally, during the execution of COFCO's fully integrated value chain, headquarters required the subsidiaries to first create their own systems to cover their business modules and applications. Simultaneous with the development, overall system integration, homogenization and synchronization with other subsidiaries should also be considered. Specifically, the ought states of the four target subsidiaries are as follows:

Womai.com might be the most unique among all COFCO subsidiaries. Womai.com is a B2C e-commerce website focusing on food products such as snacks, oils, cakes, and fruit juice. Its uniqueness primarily derives from two aspects: (1) Unlike other food-processing subsidiaries, its business does not relate to food production. Womai.com primarily concentrates on selling food products. (2) Because of Womai.com's nature as a B2C e-commerce website, it has the strongest reliance on IT of any subsidiary. Womai.com was created to provide a competitive advantage for COFCO in the e-commerce market. During our fieldwork, most of the interviewees from Womai.com's management team were IT professionals and had extensive work experience in the e-commerce industry. As one of the Senior Managers of the Strategy Department in the headquarters suggested:

"Womai.com was set up at the year of 2009 when e-commerce adoption had formed a popular market; and we were hoping to take the advantage of e-commerce website to sell our product as well. Also, the website can be viewed as a great channel of branding since we offered a specialized website for food products."

When Womai.com was established in 2009, COFCO headquarters did not consider it to be part of its fully integrated value chain strategy. The role of Womai.com was only to provide an extra channel to sell products and promote the COFCO brand to customers. More recently, during the development of the fully integrated value chain strategy and the implementation of the integrated enterprise system, headquarters realized that Womai.com could play an important role in the integrated value chain as an essential production assistant. However, due to Womai.com's initial strategic settings, it has been generally considered an isolated part that was separate from the overall value chain. Therefore, headquarters expected Womai.com to associate its business with the overall production and to export its experience in IT adoption to other subsidiaries. The Vice director of Strategy Department of the COFCO headquarters said:

"We expected Womai.com to actively participate in fully integrated value chain, and the internal resources can be therefore better used. For example, for Womai.com, it could be hard moment if the stock cannot be easily sold. Such stock can be provided to China Agri-Industries as raw material. On the other hand, China Agri-Industries can also provide Womai.com its product to lower the price and promote our brand."

As an independent firm, COFCO Tunhe is China's leading supplier of fruit and vegetable foodstuff and one of the China's largest producers of beet sugar. Its business covers the farming, processing, and trading of tomatoes, beet sugar, fruits, canned goods, and drinks. As a subsidiary of COFCO and an essential part of the fully integrated value chain strategy, COFCO Tunhe attracted a great deal of attention from COFCO headquarters. First, COFCO Tunhe is a newly merged company and it performed independently from COFCO's value chain. Secondly, when COFCO Tunhe merged into COFCO Group, it had already developed its IT systems to facilitate its production; however, the IT adoption was quite isolated in its relationship to other COFCO subsidiaries. One of the senior managers of Strategy Department of the COFCO headquarters said during the interview:

> *"Comparing to other subsidiary, the percentage and volume of COFCO Tunhe production are not so large. Therefore, we would choose COFCO Tunhe to perform its internal integrated IT system, especially for its farming, processing and producing business."*

Due to the situation at COFCO Tunhe, headquarters expected COFCO Tunhe to be the first to develop their internal integrated system. Because most of the IT adoption within COFCO Tunhe was related to food processing and production, headquarters was anxious to link this type of IT adoption to other food producing subsidiaries such as China Agri-Industries. Subsequently, COFCO Tunhe was required to align its internal systems and link them with both headquarters and other subsidiaries. As the manager of the Strategy Department of the COFCO headquarters suggested:

> *"Actually, the top management team of COFCO Tunhe attached importance to IT development since the need of their business. However, their development is comparably isolated and independent. They did not have an integrated IT system to build up the linkage of their production."*

China Foods was founded in 1990 and specialized in the production and sales of 200 types of foodstuff under the categories of chocolate, chocolate products, confectionery, and snack food. Unlike most COFCO subsidiaries, China Foods focuses on producing, packaging, and selling, and performs as the terminal of COFCO's value chain. During recent decades, China Foods had already experienced a series of IT adoptions and had integrated most of its applications. Due to its unique business, the internal integration of COFCO Food's enterprise system began with the integration and alignment of the production and marketing channels. The senior manager of the Strategy Department of the COFCO headquarters said in the interview:

> *"The ES implementation in China Foods was successful... Actually during their (China Foods) ES implementation, they performed twice. The first*

time was to perform the overall transformations of their management direc-
tion including marketing, logistics and procurement. This transformation
was prominent and inevitable for their ES implementation."

COFCO headquarters expected China Foods to play a prominent role in their development of a fully integrated value chain and ES pre-implementation. First, China Foods could be used as a successful example to show the advantages of the integrated system. Second, to execute the group level implementation, China Foods was required to continue its efforts in IT development to link their adoption with other COFCO subsidiaries. Another manager of Strategy Department of the COFCO headquarters suggested:

"ES implementation in China Foods was well done since its sensitivity in customers' needs. And we can see the overall IT development throughout the value chain, the more the subsidiaries related to dealing with customers, the more they rely on integrated systems."

Similar to COFCO Tunhe, COFCO Meat was also a newly merged firm. Its business covers feedstuff processing, livestock and poultry breeding, slaughtering, further processing, cold chain logistics, distribution, imports, and exports. However, unlike COFCO Tunhe, COFCO Meat has barely any IT applications for its business processing. However, the situation at COFCO Meat provided a perfect opportunity for headquarters to control and strategize their IT development and ES implementation. Headquarters' requirement for COFCO Meat included the following: (1) First, build their own systems to cover their business modules and applications; (2) along with this development, consider overall system integration, homogenization, and synchronization with other subsidiaries; and (3) start system development from the basic applications, which could be quickly built up. As the manager of Strategy Department of the COFCO headquarters suggested:

"We stopped one of the IT application developments of COFCO Meat last month, since it moved too fast and too independently. It couldn't be easily linked and bridged with systems from other subsidiaries."

"Our assistance (toward the system development of subsidiaries) was under conditions. We recommended our subsidiaries to adopt systems offered by the same system service provider."

Visions and Wishes from the Subsidiaries

The ideal state indicates the attributes that each subsidiary would like, ideally, to possess; it can be viewed as the ideal intention and wish of each subsidiary apart from the compulsory requirement from headquarters. Currently, most of the COFCO subsidiaries have already realized the importance of the facilitating aspects of the IT applications to their business processing. However, in the ideal state, most of them were anxious to adopt IT for their own use and neglect the linkage to other subsidiaries, which would be a tremendous obstacle to implementing integrated systems. Additionally, due to the limitations in resources and capabilities, subsidiaries must balance their business and IT development; some of them may give their business development precedence over the corporate-level fully integrated value chain strategy.

As mentioned above, Womai.com was established to be a B2C e-commerce website and an extra channel through which COFCO could reinforce its competitive advantage and promote its brand to a broader customer group. Unlike most COFCO subsidiaries, the management team at Womai.com was constituted by IT professionals rather than executives in the food processing business. Therefore, during COFCO's ES pre-implementation, Womai.com still regarded itself as a pure B2C e-commerce website, and its business goals were more related to online selling and marketing. Specifically, to maintain market share in the food e-commerce industry, Womai.com also sold products from other food-processing companies, even COFCO's major competitors. Therefore, in the ideal state, Womai. com did not intend to dedicate themselves to the development of the fully integrated value chain and integrated ES implementation. The current desires and vision for Womai.com remained to maintain competitiveness through technology innovation and e-commerce strategy transformation. General Manager of Womai.com said during the interview:

"We did not consider ourselves as a part in the traditional COFCO value chain... Currently, our focus remains at selling products. The products

include not only COFCO products, but also products with other brand. We cannot survive in the market if we are not doing so."

Also, the IT Director of Womai.com also suggested:

"At beginning, though theoretically Womai.com is a part of COFCO Group, the operation is quite so different. We cannot adapt the thinking pattern of COFCO to run Womai.com. For example, selling product online has its unique rules which we have to learn and adapt from e-commerce industry such as review and rating. Also it (e-commerce industry) requires special promotion approach for products."

Similar to Womai.com's isolation in COFCO, as a newly merged company, COFCO Tunhe also did not pay much attention to the integrated ES implementation. However, unlike Womai.com, the development of an integrated system in COFCO Tunhe was impeded by business dynamism stemming from the production processes at COFCO Tunhe. COFCO Tunhe owned several production lines including tomatoes, beets, and fruits. Each of these lines requires a unique processing approach and timing. It is difficult to integrate this type of complex production into a single internal system. Furthermore, COFCO Tunhe had already adopted its IT to its unique business dynamics; this IT system would be difficult to integrate and link with other subsidiaries. Specifically, the system software they adopted was different from those adopted by other subsidiaries. Therefore, although the management team of COFCO Tunhe wanted to build their own IT applications for the production lines, they did not intend to consider the issues of integration — neither among their internal production lines nor with other subsidiaries. As VP of COFCO Tunhe suggested in our interview:

"I do not think the development of fully integrated chain will be executed very smoothly throughout COFCO. To me, it is a mission impossible and I do not hear the president mention it all the time during the top management team meeting... Currently, I certainly want to build up our own IT applications for our own business; however our business dynamics do not allow us to consider the overall integration with other subsidiaries. It is enough difficult for us to build our own enterprise systems."

It has been widely acknowledged in the COFCO Group that the ES implementation in China Foods was a great success. The sensitivity to customer service led China Foods to focus significant attention to IT development in facilitating their business. The role played by China Foods during the overall ES implementation was emphasized and promoted by the headquarters to the other subsidiaries. China Foods wished to continue developing their internal IT applications and to export their experience in ES implementation. As the Manager of IT Department of COFCO said in the interview:

"We are proud of our ERP development, and we wish to continue reconstruction our business process to coordinate ES development. Now we would like to export our experience in ERP implementation during the past 5–6 years."

VP of China Foods also suggested:

"Our process is complex and the ERP implementation needs the coordination through our entire department which is a difficulty during implementation. Now we wish our emphasis in ERP implementation would play an important role in business process and to better accomplish the requirements (in production, sales, and revenue) from the headquarters."

COFCO Meat was also a newly merged company. However, unlike COFCO Tunhe, it had very few IT applications for its business. At the same time, COFCO Meat lacked the resources and capabilities to execute an ES implementation. COFCO Meat wanted to take advantage of the opportunity to create an internal integrated system as well as to establish an IT team for their own use. Because COFCO Meat was eager to use IT to facilitate their business, they could possibly neglect integration. As VP and financial director of COFCO Meat indicated their response to the requirement from the headquarters:

"Our process is complex and the ERP implementation needs the coordination through our entire department which is a difficulty during implementation. Now we wish our emphasis in ERP implementation would play an important role in business process and to better accomplish the requirements (in production, sales, and revenue) from the headquarters."

Current States of the Subsidiaries

The actual state represents the attributes that each of the subsidiaries believes it actually possesses, which may be different from what headquarters wants it to possess or what it ideally wants to possess. Due to limited resources and the capability and complexity of business dynamisms, the subsidiaries had to balance between IT and business development; at the same time, it may be excessively difficult for some of the subsidiaries to consider overall integration. Generally, most of COFCO's subsidiaries prioritized themselves when addressing the requirements from the headquarters for the integrated ES implementation and its development for business processes.

Womai.com was an extra channel through which COFCO promoted its brand and attracted a broader customer range online. However, during the past five years, the e-commerce industry in China had substantially transformed. Tremendous competition in the B2C market made it excessively difficult for e-commerce companies to survive. In particular, Womai.com's products remained purely food-related, but several competitors had emerged in this market during recent years, who offered a greater variety of products that extended beyond food-related products. Under these fierce and drastic circumstances, Womai.com had to put its survival above the overall integrated enterprise system. At the same time, within Womai.com, there was a high density of IT applications due to the nature of the e-commerce website; COFCO headquarters wanted Womai.com to export its experience in the IT development and IT adoption to the other subsidiaries. However, the isolated state of Womai.com made it almost impossible for it to participate in other units and projects. As the General Manager of Womai.com suggested in the interview:

"We have more than 300 employees in Womai.com and a strong team in IT. Also, some of our executive teams are made of marketing personnel (in relating to online marketing)... We don't see us any common with other traditional COFCO subsidiaries. You see, we are IT professionals and online marketing personnel, we know nothing about planting, farming, food producing and etc."

The Marketing Director of Womai.com also indicated their current difficulty:

"Nowadays there is enough trouble for us to deal with the online competitors. We need to expend our market share to survive in the e-commerce industry. Our responsibility is to maintain the annual revenue, which is also a compulsory requirement from the headquarters. We don't see how the fully integrated value chain could help us on that."

Similar to the isolated state of Womai.com, COFCO Tunhe also appeared to be cloistered from the other food processing and producing subsidiaries to some extent. Specifically, due to the complexity of their business dynamics and their several production lines, COFCO Tunhe emphasized developing IT applications customized to their business processes. Because of the uniqueness of each production line, COFCO Tunhe felt no need to establish an integrated system to facilitate overall control. Further, the lack of IT resources also constricted COFCO Tunhe's intention to participate in group-level integration. COFCO Tunhe owned several elementary IT applications to separately facilitate their production lines and did not aspire to integrate them or incorporate them with the overall ES implementation. As the VP of COFCO Veges indicated:

"Our production lines are so unique and we spend much efforts to maintain it perform smoothly. For example, tomato production line alone costs us a great deal of attention. You see, the farming of tomato depends much on the weather. If the rain is not enough, the tomato would not fulfill the standard in making ketchup. Also, the timing is also so important, without calculating on weather and timing, tomatoes would rot so quickly during producing. Similar things happened in beet and fruit production lines. That's why we cannot integrate them so easily."

As we mentioned earlier, China Foods had the most successful experience in ES implementation and IT development. The business of China Foods required it to react sensitively to customers' needs and to coordinate and generally control every part of its production lines. In this sense, China Foods began its IT development 10 years ago and had integrated most of its applications internally. More recently, increasingly intense competition had led China Foods to consider cooperating with other subsidiaries, especially those relating to food production and processing, such as China Agri-Industries and COFCO Tunhe. For example, China Foods was conducting group-level database development, which required facilitation from China Agri-Industries and the other food-producing subsidiaries. China Foods, as the "final exit" of the integrated value chain, was the most capable of these subsidiaries in integrating its internal production data. The Director of the Financial Department of China Foods suggested in the interview:

"Currently, although comparing to other subsidiaries, we have better accomplishment in IT development, we still need to develop new systems to solve the problem we found during our experience. Also, as the president, as well as the headquarters has higher expectations to us, we are refining our systems and IT application more meticulous and strict."

The VP of China Foods also indicated their difficulty during the interview that:

"Though we are ahead of others (other COFCO subsidiaries), our current systems and IT applications still need to refine and rearrange. Our business process is also complex and so many participants (within China Foods) need to involve in our ES implementation. I admit we have already got a series of IT application and enterprise system, it is not yet perfect."

The business process of COFCO Meat included livestock and poultry breeding, slaughtering, further processing, and cold chain logistics, which required conformity and alignment among each IT module. However, the dynamics of its business process, such as the preservation of meat and the high standard of logistics, made it complicated to develop IT applications. Another difficulty for COFCO Meat was its IT resources and capabilities; its development of IT applications had started rather late compared to the other subsidiaries, and there were barely any IT applications relating to its business processes before 2011. In incorporating IT adoptions for the needs of the business process,

COFCO Meat was anxious to participate in the development of an over-all ES implementation to gain support from headquarters and for its own use. However, though it is a benefit to be facilitated by the headquarters, COFCO Meat was not so enthusiastic in linking its own business to other subsidiaries. As one of the Employees from the Strategy Department of the COFCO headquarters responded:

> *"COFCO Meat's IT development started quite late comparing to other subsidiaries. Now they are working on the project of EIP. However, China Foods began with EIP from 2006 and they've already finished reconstruction by last year."*

VP and financial director of COFCO Meat also indicated their difficulty in lacking of IT capabilities and resources that:

> *"At the beginning, we only had 2 full-time employees covering the IT development and adoption for the whole company."*

The difficulty for COFCO headquarters in implementing their integrated enterprise systems remained in the cultural differences in attitudes toward integrated systems and IT applications among the subsidiaries. These differences derived from the discrepancies among subsidiaries in terms of their values and opinions regarding the integrated ES project and their priorities in terms of spending their limited resources on IT develop-ment versus addressing business dynamics. The discrepancy in IT capa-bilities triggered differences in operating routines among the subsidiaries. Some subsidiaries, despite their willingness and anxiety to implement integrated enterprise systems, were restricted by the development of their IT applications and capabilities, which could potentially jeopardize the implementation and hold back the project schedule. The dissolution of these discrepancies — the cultural differences based on value and routine toward the integrated ES implementation — could be recognized as the goal of headquarters' culture retooling. Therefore, during the pre-implementation stage, the primary task for COFCO headquarters was to identify the discrepancies of each subsidiary and, accordingly, enact the cultural retooling approach and strategy.

References

Branigan, T. "Chinese Figures Show Fivefold Rise in Babies Sick from Contaminated Milk," *The Guardian*, (2) 2008, pp. 12.
Development Research Center of the State Council. "Analysis Report of Food Processing Industry in China 2011–2012", 2012.

Discussion Questions

1. What are the difficulties of COFCO subsidiaries in implementing integrated enterprise systems?
2. How are the difficulties of subsidiaries encountered during implementing the integrated enterprise system different from each other?
3. What problems can be anticipated during the implementation of integrated systems? What are the key challenges of COFCO headquarters in implementing their integrated enterprise systems?
4. If you are the CIO of COFCO Group, what will you do during the pre-implementation stage to be sure of the readiness of each of the subsidiaries?

Index

.

Printed in the United States
By Bookmasters